The New Americans
Recent Immigration and American Society

Edited by
Steven J. Gold and Rubén G. Rumbaut

A Series from LFB Scholarly

Language, Gender, and Academic Performance
A Study of the Children of Dominican Immigrants

Flavia C. Peréa

LFB Scholarly Publishing LLC
El Paso 2011

Library of Congress Cataloging-in-Publication Data

Peréa, Flavia C.
  Language, gender, and academic performance : a study of the children
of Dominican immigrants / Flavia C. Peréa.
    p. cm. -- (The new Americans: recent Immigration and American
society)
  Includes bibliographical references and index.
  ISBN 978-1-59332-390-5 (hardcover : alk. paper)
  1. Children of immigrants--Education--United States--Case studies. 2.
Children of immigrants--Language--United States--Case studies. 3.
Native language and education--United States--Case studies. 4.
Bilingual education--United States--Case studies. 5. Sex differences in
education--United States--Case studies. 6. Dominicans (Dominican
Republic)--United States--Social conditions. I. Title.
  LC3746.P45 2011
  370.117'50973--dc22
                                        2011002364

ISBN 978-1-59332-390-5

Printed on acid-free 250-year-life paper.

Manufactured in the United States of America.

For Daddy

Table of Contents

List of Tables ix

List of Figures xi

Acknowledgements xiii

Foreword by Cynthia García Coll xv

CHAPTER 1: Introduction 1

CHAPTER 2: Dominican Immigrants in the US and Providence, Rhode Island 9

CHAPTER 3: What do we know about Children of Immigrant Families? 17

CHAPTER 4: Guiding Theories 47

CHAPTER 5: The Nuts and Bolts of this Study 55

CHAPTER 6: Modeling Language, Gender, and Academic Performance 71

CHAPTER 7: So what does all this Mean? 105

CHAPTER 8: Closing Thoughts 119

Notes 129

Appendix A 131

References 135

Index 147

List of Tables

Table 1: Providence School Demographics, School Year 2009-2010,
by grade level (percentages) 15

Table 2: Example of Scoring for Composite Score of Language
Preference Measure 60

Table 3: Sample Distribution by Sex and Cohort 71

Table 4: Child's Place of Birth and Parents' Place of Birth,
by Sex and Cohort (percentages) 72

Table 5: Mother's Language(s) and Language(s)
Spoken in the Home (percentages) 72

Table 6: Childs Primary Language Preference Distribution
(percentages) 73

Table 7: Distribution of Grades (percentages) 75

Table 8: Annual and Three Year Average Grade Point Average
(GPA) 75

Table 9: Language Preference and Three Year Grade Point Average
(GPA) 76

Table 10: Mean Differences: Language Preference and Three Year
Grade Point Average (GPA) 78

Table 11: Mean Differences: Language Preference and Grade Point
Average (GPA) for Year 2 79

Table 12: Correlations: Children's Characteristics and English
Preference 82

Table 13: Multivariate Regression: Predictors of Academic
Achievement 86

Table 14: Multivariate Regression: Bilingual Preference
as a Predictor of Academic Achievement for Boys and Girls 87

Table 15: Multivariate Regression Grouped by Sex: English
Preference as a Predictor of Academic Achievement for Boys
and Girls 88

Table 16: Predictive Value of Bilingual Language Preference over
Three Years 91

Table 17: Predictive Value of Bilingual Language Preference over
Three Years, by Sex 92

List of Figures

Figure 1: Theoretical model 67

Figure 2: Latent variable: Academic Performance 94

Figure 3: Latent variable: Child Bilingual Preference 95

Figure 4: Latent variable: Mother's Language use and Comfort 96

Figure 5: Final Structural Equation Model: Child Bilingual
Preference and Academic Performance 99

Figure 6: Final Structural Equation Model: Girls' Bilingual
Preference and Academic Performance. 100

Acknowledgements

This book would not have been possible without the tremendous support, encouragement, and love I have received from so many special and wonderful people.

To Cynthia García Coll: thank you for opening the door and for pulling me through. I would not be where I am today if I hadn't met you at just the right time. Thank you for welcoming me into your research team, for access to the CIDC data, and for your insights, honesty, patience, love, enthusiasm and inexhaustible support.

Thank you so much to Rubén Rumbaut and Steven Gold for taking an interest in my research, and for shepherding me through this entire process. Thank you for reading so many versions of this manuscript, and for your invaluable edits and comments which helped me to strengthen this book tremendously. Thank you to Leo Balk at LFB Scholarly Publishing for your patience and for making this book happen. A warm thank you to Carola Suarez-Orozco, for your interest, excitement, and for connecting the dots to make this book possible.

To Lorraine Klerman, Grant Ritter, and Tom Shapiro, thank you for your guidance and help throughout the course of this study. This would not have been possible without you.

Many thanks to Linda Martinez for being a wonderful research partner and collaborator. To Amy Kerivan Marks and Flannery Patton, thank you for being great company to do my research.

Thank you to my undergraduate student assistants, Chloe Dillaway and Dana Harada at Tufts University, for their invaluable assistance during the final stages of this project. Thank you for your tireless and thorough work helping me to finalize the manuscript and ensure it was good to go to press!

Thank you to the Spencer Foundation and the Heller Alumni Annual Fund at Brandeis University for some very much appreciated financial support.

To Sean, thank you for sticking by my side throughout this journey. You're my anchor.

Thank you to my family and my father especially. Daddy: Thank you for preparing me to be everything that I am. I miss you so much. I wish you could be here. I hope I've made you proud.

Foreword
by Cynthia García Coll

The process of immigration is as old as humans creating permanent settlements. Poverty, displacement, famine and persecution have been common antecedents of migration across history. The dreams and plans for the future are powerful, as captured by Fievel, the child of the mouse family immigrating to the United States in the movie An American Tale "there are no cats in America and the streets are paved with cheese!" But there have always been required adaptations to different climates, geographies, languages, customs and rituals. Reality bites. And struggles ensue as different family members work through acculturating to a new land, in different ways, as immigrants have at different times throughout human history.

In many occasions, families migrate so the next generation has a better chance at life. The parents sacrifice the familiar, their networks, the value of their skills and knowledge for the unknown. Sometimes they are surprised and alarmed at how much more difficult things are in the new country. But, as revealed in many stories of immigration, if the children are adapting well, parents feel the sacrifices made are worth it.

For many of these children, succeeding in school means repaying their elders for their sacrifices, but it is also their only way out of poverty and increasing their social status. Doing well in school is their job; their employment. Most parents have high expectations for their children: Over 90% of mothers expect their children to go to college and become professionals such as physicians, engineers and lawyers (Garcia Coll et al, 2002; Garcia Coll & Marks, 2009). Similarly, Asian and Latino immigrant students report very positive attitudes toward teachers, school work and the institution (Fuligni, 1997; Suarez-Orozco & Suarez-Orozco, 1995). However, these attitudes are related to

xv

similarly positive academic outcomes (GPA, test scores) in Asians, but not always among Latinos-why?

This book, by Dr. Flavia Peréa, represents one of the first attempts to answer this question for a very recent newcomer group, children of families from Dominican Republic. Although rather close geographically to Puerto Rico and Cuba, these three Islands have dramatically different political and immigration histories in relation to the United States. Regardless of the differences, Diaspora from the three Islands have come here and remain in the United States. Initially settling into ethnic enclaves in Florida and New York, they have slowly dispersed all over the nation. What they also have in common is the basic experience of having to acculturate to North American culture, a story that has become more complicated as scholars like Dr. Peréa have dug into it.

Dr. Peréa started her enquiry into the role of language by positing that language acculturation would be one of the mechanisms by which we could understand individual differences in academic performance among Dominican children in the United States. It is important to remember that the children she studied are from Dominican families who have immigrated to the U.S. relatively recently; the children are second generation between the ages of six and twelve and studied longitudinally, a great data set to for these enquiries.

Her main hypothesis reflects a paradigm shift in how we conceptualize the role of language acquisition and loss of the native language in academic success. The traditional view of immersion (English only) and assimilation (leave your language and culture behind) has a long history in this country, with analysis of policies toward bilingual education in this country representing tremendous, perhaps cyclical shifts since its inception to the present day (Peréa & García Coll, 2008). Traditionally, the assumption is that the quicker you learn English the better you will do academically. If you lose your native language, that is irrelevant and often considered a positive outcome. But that is not what Dr. Peréa is posing. She is proposing bilingualism is an asset for children of immigrant families and associated with academic success. For her, fluency in each language contributes to academic endeavors. Thus her argument rests on a variety of key findings (Feliciano, 2001; Portes and Rumbaut, 2001; Rumbaut, 1995; Suarez-Orozco & Suarez-Orozco, 1995) and theories

(Fillmore, 1991; LaFromboise, 1993), which argue that children in immigrant families learning English is as important as retaining their families' native languages. Why could that be?

- Because learning academic English takes time, 5 to 7 years, and in the meantime learning in both languages can reinforce the learning process.
- Because learning one language well first provides the bases for learning another.
- Because children who maintain their native language do not lose the support of an extended family system.
- Because these children can develop a positive ethnic/racial identity which can be protective especially, when they confront racism, or discrimination.

Her hypothesis, however, is only partially supported by her findings in ways that beg for good theoretical explanations. It is true that bilingual preference among Dominican children is significantly positively correlated with 3 year GPA, whereas English preference is negatively correlated. In other words children who are more acculturated and prefer English over Spanish or bilingualism do worse in school. However, when gender differences are examined, strong moderation of this association by sex between bilingualism and GPA is found. The association is present and strong for girls and not for boys. As with any good piece of research, some questions are answered and others arise. Why would being bilingualism appear as a protective factor for girls and not boys? Dr, Peréa's interpretation of the results emphasizes the non-uniform or linear nature of acculturation processes, how and why they may vary within large pan-ethnic or distinct ethnic/national groups. As such, her research highlights the need for within group studies that take into account the various contextual influences at work, and the importance of weighing these when trying to better understand developmental processes and outcomes among new immigrant groups- but you have to read the book!

The beauty of this book is the richness of the data and the systematic step-by-step approach to the analysis. The book remains focused to the question that it addresses. It also examines the literature systematically to inform not only its basic hypothesis, but the explanation of unexpected results. By looking at only one immigrant group with three levels of increasingly sophisticated and complementary analysis, Dr. Peréa has amassed a deep knowledge of the distinct characteristics of this particular group, and its commonalities and differences from other minority and immigrant groups.

The universal processes and characteristics of immigration are present in this one story of immigration and acculturation- what immigrants bring with them, the assets and vulnerabilities these present for their children, and this one group's particular context of reception in the U.S. These represent major variables. But one must keep in mind these are also children and families doing the best they can, often in the face of trying circumstances, holding dreams and aspirations. But what immigrants and their children encounter once they arrive in this socially stratified country can determine opportunities or the lack thereof, and shape the pathways they are set upon, pathways that can vary based on language, race/ethnicity, or gender.

This a Dominican Diaspora at the beginning of the 21st century, and like earlier waves of immigration it will come and go. Some will integrate into the mainstream, others will not. But these are lives that because of this book we understand better, which we hope will help us to support them in their quest to make it in the United States. After all there ARE cats in America and the streets are NOT paved with gold!

CHAPTER 1
Introduction

Throughout U.S. history, immigration has played a significant role in shaping the social, cultural, and political landscape of this country. Although Native Peoples were present within the present-day political borders of the U.S. before the arrival of the Europeans, and African Peoples were brought to the Americas as slaves who did not chose to immigrate; it is immigration, voluntary or under duress, that arguably has had the greatest effect on the demographic composition of this country. Although, in its entirety, the U.S. is not solely a country of immigrants, the U.S. as we know it is a country that was founded by immigrants, and immigration remains as decisive and divisive an issue today at the turn of the millennium as it has been throughout U.S. history.

The dramatic population changes currently unfolding are arguably the defining issue of the times as they are affecting every facet of life in this country. Immigrants represented 12.5 percent of the U.S. population in 2008, of whom 43 percent were naturalized citizens, an increase from 11.7 percent in 2003 (Larsen, 2004). This reflects the rapid growth of the foreign-born demographic which has more than tripled since the 1970s when it was 4.7 percent (Fix and Passel, 2003), and which is as close to the high of 14.8 percent reached in 1890. Immigration has become the decisive factor in the growth and change of the U.S. population, as demographic changes are primarily driven by a steady increase in immigration, which have been exacerbated by a relative decrease (aging and decreased birth rates) among the majority white non-Latino demographic. Immigration to the US, which is primarily from Latin America and to a lesser degree Asia, has been driving profound changes in the racial/ethnic composition of the US population in the last ~45 years. 1965 is an important milestone in US immigration policy because it was the year the US government amended the Immigration Act , repealing the national origins quota system and replacing it with a system based on family reunification, and with a focus on attracting immigrants with needed skills to the US. It was the most extensive revision of US immigration policy since the 1920s.

Because the U.S. is adjacent to Latin America, and because of the unique historical political, and economic relationship between the U.S. and Latin American countries, the new immigration since 1965 is primarily from within the hemisphere . In 2007 more than half (53.6%) of the US foreign born population was from Latin America, of which more than two-thirds were immigrants from Mexico and Central America who alone accounted for more than one third of the total foreign-born (Grieco, 2009). However, it is important to note that not all Latinos are immigrants. Although 39.8 percent of Latinos are foreign born compared to 12.6% of the overall US population, the majority of Latinos (60%) are born in the US and thus not immigrants, but native-born US citizens. Therefore, Latinos are a diverse population that is immigrant, migrant and native-born,

High immigration from Latin America combined with the high birth rates, has caused the Latino population in this country to grow steadily and greatly. According to 2006-2008 American Community Survey (ACS) estimates, Latinos comprise 15.1 percent of the population, making Latinos the largest minority group in the U.S. (Blacks and Asians account for 12.3% and 4.4%, respectively). Although the total U.S. population grew by 13 percent during the 1990s, the Latino population experienced a significantly faster growth rate of 61 percent during that period. This trend is projected to continue as the Latino population grows steadily throughout the twenty-first century. By 2050 the Latino population is projected to triple and its share of the total population to double and account for a projected 30 percent. Thus, by mid-century approximately one in three US residents would be Latino. The Latino population is expected to continue growing past 2100 and continue to grow thereafter. Therefore, Latinos are and will remain the largest minority and ethnic group in the U.S. well into the future.

The growth of the Latino population presents certain challenges and questions about how to best integrate this population into the socio-cultural, economic and political fabric of this country. In 2004 most Latinos spoke only English at home (22.8%) or did not speak English at home but spoke English very well (38.5%). Although not all Latinos speak Spanish, the US has a large Spanish speaking population and more than 75 percent of Latinos speak Spanish, many of whom are monolingual Spanish speakers. In 2000, of the 47 million people in the US who spoke a language other than English, more than half (59.8%) spoke Spanish. Many, but not all, Latinos are Spanish-English bilinguals. Of more than 75 percent who spoke a language other than English effectively all (99%) spoke Spanish. 38.7 percent of Latinos reported speaking English less than very well, much more than the 8.1 percent of the total US population. As these numbers indicate, the number of bilingual and monolingual Spanish speakers is large, and as the Latino population grows steadily over the century this trend will continue.

The Latino population is a young demographic with high birth rates. The median age for Latinos was 26.9 in 2004, thirteen years younger than that of non-Latino whites (40.1 years), and one in three Latinos is a child under 18, illustrating the youthfulness of the population. Latino children accounted for 17% of all children under age 18. This means that Latino children constitute a small, but nevertheless greater percent of the population under 18 than Latinos as a group account for in the total US population, illustrating the young age of the population. Latino children will soon constitute largest segment of the overall child population, as it is projected that 39% of all children (<18 years) will be Latino by midcentury.

The high fertility rates illustrate why births are outpacing immigration as the main source of Latino population growth . Children of immigrants (the second generation) are the fastest growing sub-population of U.S. children (Hernandez, 2004) and Latino children accounted for 17 percent of all children under age 18 (Lugalia & Overturf, 2003), the vast majority of whom are Latino. In 2000 more than half (56%) of children living with a foreign-born householder were Latino. Clearly, the spheres where demographic changes stand to have the greatest impact are in the areas that serve children, such as schools.

The impact of immigration and the parallel growth of the Latino population are perhaps most strikingly evident in our schools.

Although the majority of students (58%) were US-born non-Latino white students, Latinos, as well as Blacks, were the largest minority groups enrolled in U.S. schools among the native population in 2006, each comprising 14 percent. Latino students make up increasing proportions of the school age population. Between 1988 and 2008, the percentage of Latino students doubled from 11 to 22 percent, and in 2008, Latino enrollment exceeded 10 million students (Aud, et al., 2010). The foreign born comprised 7 percent of the student population in 2006, of which 3 percent was Latino (Davis & Bauman, 2008). On average, 22 percent of all students had at least one foreign-born parent in 2006, as did 66 percent of Latino children in 2003 (18% were foreign born themselves and 47% US-born) (Shin, 2005).

The number of school-age children ages 5-17 who spoke a language other than English at home has increased from 3.8 to 10.9 million between 1979 and 2008, or from 9 to 21 percent of this age group, and from 18 to 21percent between 2000 and 2008 (Aud, et al., 2010). Mirroring their representation in the overall population and steady population growth, children who speak a language other than English in their homes were, are, and will continue to be overwhelmingly Spanish speaking Latinos .

In 2005, 6.9 million Latino students (69.8%) spoke a language other than English at home, of whom 19.1 percent spoke English with difficulty (Kewal Ramani, et al., 2007). Of students age 5 and older in 2006, 21 percent spoke a language other than English at home, of whom 16 percent spoke English very well and 5 percent spoke English less than very well in 2006. Spanish was the predominant language spoken by 13.5 percent of students (Davis & Bauman, 2008). In 2006, students who spoke a language other than English in their homes comprised 20 percent of students in nursery school and kindergarten, and 21 percent of students in grades 1-12. Of this 20 percent, 13.5 percent were Spanish speakers comprising 15 percent of children in nursery school, kindergarten, and grades 1-12 (Davis & Bauman, 2008). In 2008, some 21 percent of children ages 5–17 (or 10.9 million) spoke a language other than English at home. Of these, 5 percent (or 2.7 million) spoke English with difficulty and 75 percent were Spanish speakers. Seventeen percent of school age Latino students who spoke Spanish at home also had difficulty speaking English (Aud, et al., 2010). These trends among students in US schools area expected to continue well into the future. The Census Bureau predicts that by the 2030s children who speak a language other than English at home will constitute 40 percent of the school-age population.

Given the size, youthfulness, and high fertility rate of the Latino population, understanding the determinants of educational outcomes is particularly important as regards Latino children. Latino children face various risk factors and barriers to educational advancement. Although Hispanic parents report having the same high expectations for their child's educational attainment as all other population groups, Latinos are the least educated population in the U.S., with only 11% receiving a bachelor's degree by the age of 25 compared to 17% of Blacks, 30% of Whites, and 49% of Asian Americans in the same age group (Schneider, Martinez & Owens, 2006). Parents' low educational attainment and socioeconomic status, which is often complicated by a lack of U.S. citizenship and/or knowledge about the US education system, often leads to an early disadvantage for Latino children that is proving difficult to overcome. The disadvantage accumulates over time, starting with Latino children being less-likely to enroll in preschool, a lack of literary activities within the home, as well as teacher bias in kindergarten against the academic potential of Latino children (Schneider, Martinez & Owens, 2006). These factors can perhaps help to understand why bilingual students are most at risk for placement in a remedial program. Because academic pathways are established early, academic underperformance continues from elementary school through middle school and follows most students into high school. Poor connections between teachers and Latino students can exacerbate the difficulties transitioning from middle school to high school. Better understanding of the assets and vulnerabilities Latino students have and bring to their education is important to help stem the tide of poor educational performance among Latino students; given current demographic projections it is arguably necessary in order to avert a long lasting national catastrophe with profound implications for our society and economy, and if the US is to maintain its standing in the world, a primary reason it attracts large numbers of immigrants in the first place.

The growth among the immigrant population, especially those from Latin America , has raised concerns about their ability to acculturate, enter the U.S. mainstream, and become "American". In particular, one of the most contentious issues current demographic changes raise is English language acquisition, in particular with regard to Spanish speakers. English is by far the dominant language of this country and is essentially required to "make it". Research suggests that today's Spanish-speaking immigrants are learning English as quickly as earlier European immigrants (Rodriguez, 2001). The linguistic assimilation of immigrants has been documented, and new evidence is confirming what linguists have argued for decades: the first generation is monolingual, the second bilingual, and the third is either English monolingual or prefers English. Some scholars have even suggested that assimilation and a shift to English language dominance among immigrants, especially Spanish speakers, is growing and rapidly approaching a two-generation pattern (Rodriguez, 2001; Veltman, 1983, 1988 [as cited in Crawford, 2000. p. 6]).

However, one subject of fierce debate is whether learning English should come at the expense of losing the native language, and if preservation of the native language compromises people's ability to learn English. The idea that merely speaking a "foreign" language other than English is itself a liability is clearly pervasive in mainstream culture and is concurrent with anti-immigrant sentiments today. However, the other question the language and immigrant integration issue raises (and which, in light of emerging evidence, is being asked with greater frequency,) is whether maintenance of the native language is an asset that can function as a protective factor, and if losing it poses certain risks for immigrants and their children as they adjust to life in this country. This is particularly an issue for school-age children of immigrant families, who must adapt to life in the US as American children of immigrants. Greater use of English among immigrants has historically been regarded as a positive advancement, an indication that immigrants are integrating, moving up the socioeconomic ladder, and becoming "American". However, as will be discussed, research on children of immigrant families has found that greater use of English may not necessarily be a positive development, as evidence suggests that assimilation, or greater/more acculturation, and increased use of English may have a negative effect on academic performance, as well as other outcomes.

The impact of current demographic changes is evident in cities, the suburbs, rural areas, and in every facet of life in this country. These changes transcend socioeconomic and racial/ethnic borders as no aspect of U.S. society is immune to the effects of these profound population changes. Whether one is in "favor" of or "opposed" to immigration today at the dawn of the 21st Century, and whether one sees the so-called "Latinization" of the U.S. as an asset or a threat to the socio-cultural fabric of this country; the fact remains that immigration has historically had, is having, and will continue to have a profound impact on U.S. society, and Latinos as a group will play a decisive role in shaping the future. Although the implementation of restrictive immigration policies could stem the tide of immigrants, there is nothing that can alter the number of US-born second-generation children of immigrants who are already here. Thus, as was the case with Italian, Irish, and German immigrants at the turn of the twentieth century, Latin American immigrants today will be instrumental in shaping the future of the nation. Because health and economic advancement are intimately tied to educational achievement, the success of their children in school is crucial.

CHAPTER 2

Dominican Immigrants in the US and Providence, Rhode Island

Dominicans are presently the fifth largest Latino national group in the US, comprising 2.6 percent of the Latino population in 2007. Between 1990 and 2000 the US-born Dominican population grew at a faster rate than the foreign-born, however the majority of growth among the Dominican population was due to immigration (Migration Policy Institute, 2004). Growth among the foreign-born segment of the population accounts for 63 percent of total growth, highlighting that Dominican population growth is largely driven by immigration (Migration Policy Institute, 2004). Between 2000 and 2010 the Dominican population is projected to increase by 41 percent (Migration Policy Institute, 2004).

Because of the historic im/migration patterns of Latinos from the Caribbean to the mainland U.S., Dominicans are primarily concentrated in south Florida and the northeast, particularly in urban areas such New York City, NY, Boston, MA, Providence, RI, and Hartford, CT. In the northeast and the New England region Caribbean Latinos represent the largest segment of the Latino population. The majority of Dominicans (82%) live in the northeast, of which more than half live in the New York metro region (Migration Policy Institute, 2004). Among the five U.S. states with Dominican populations over 20,000, Rhode Island, along with Florida, experienced the most rapid growth between 1990 and 2000 (Migration Policy Institute, 2004). Dominicans are the third largest immigrant group in New England (Marcuss & Borgos, 2004), and between 1990 and 2000 the Dominican population in the states of Massachusetts and Rhode Island more than doubled (Migration Policy Institute, 2004). Rhode Island had the fastest growing Dominican population, increasing by 168 percent (Migration Policy Institute, 2004). Of the total U.S. Dominican population 2.4 percent lives in RI and is concentrated in the Providence-Fall River-Pawtucket, Massachusetts and Rhode Island region, which ranks eighth among U.S. metropolitan regions with the largest Dominican populations (Migration Policy Institute, 2004). These figures reflect the high rate of migration from the island to the mainland, and the importance of Rhode Island and specifically Providence as a destination and settlement point for Dominican immigrants.

Demographic Profile

Characteristic of the Dominican Republic's Afro-Caribbean history, over 85 percent of Dominicans are of African ancestry (Bailey, 2002). Thus, Dominicans are Black in the US racial context, and therefore, more often than not, will be raced black in the U.S. Dominicans have slightly higher levels of educational attainment compared to the Latino population overall. Fifteen percent of Dominicans ages 25 and older have earned at least a bachelor's degree, compared to 12.6% among all Latinos. This reflects the characteristics of Dominicans who migrate to the US from the island. Dominican immigrants to the US starting in the late 1960's were primarily lower-middle and middle-class from the cities, not from the interior of the island or the countryside, and thus from the skilled and better educated sectors of Dominican society. However, although Dominican immigrants in the US have higher levels of education compared to the overall population of the Dominican Republic, they are not well educated by U.S. standards (Bailey, 2000). According to the 2005-2007 American Community Survey 3-year estimates, a mere 62.9% of Dominicans graduate from high school in the U.S. as opposed to 84% of non-Latino whites. The educational characteristics of Dominicans helps to explain the relatively low socioeconomic status of Dominicans in the U.S. compared to all Latinos. In the northeastern U.S., Caribbean Latinos experience poverty at greater levels than any other Latino ethnic group (Falcon, Tucker, & Bermudez, 1997). In 2007 Dominicans earned comparably less as the median annual income for those ages 16 and older was $20,238 compared to $21,048 among all US Latinos. Dominicans have double the rate of poverty, 24.2 percent, compared to 11.9 percent among the general U.S. population, which is also higher than the 19.5 poverty rate among all Latinos. Dominicans are also less likely to own their own home, 27.9 percent compared to 49.9 percent among Latinos as a whole and 67.2 percent among the general US population.

Although Dominicans are demographically similar to the overall Latino population, there are characteristics that distinguish Dominicans from other Latinos. Sixty percent of Dominicans are foreign born and almost half (46.3%) of immigrants are U.S. citizens. Dominicans are younger than the U.S. population and older than Hispanics overall. The median age of Dominicans is 29, compared to 27 among all Latinos and 36 among the total US population. Although the Latino population has higher rates of marriage and more two-parent families compared to the U.S. white and Black populations, Dominicans are less likely to be married than Latinos overall, 37.5 percent compared to 47.3 percent. Dominican women ages 15 to 44 also have higher rates of unmarried births (49.9%) compared to all Latina (38.1%) and all U.S women (33.4%) (Pew Hispanic Center, 2009).

A majority of Dominicans (52.2%) speak English proficiently, although almost half of Dominicans ages 5 and older (47.8%) report speaking English less than very well compared to 38.8% of all Hispanics. Among Dominican children, however, a whopping 88 percent spoke Spanish at home in 2005 (Kewal Ramani, et al., 2007).

Immigration from the Dominican Republic

Dominicans are a relatively new immigrant community, as most immigrants from the Dominican Republic (56.5%) came to the U.S. in 1990 or later (Pew Hispanic Center, 2009). Most Dominican immigrants to the U.S. came under the Family Reunification provisions of the 1965 Immigration and Naturalization Act. Therefore, there are familial and social networks and supports already present in the receiving country. Family ties are important aspects of migration, which in the case of Dominicans are structurally built into the migration process (Bailey, 2000).

Immigration today is distinct from earlier waves of U.S. immigration because immigrants today maintain close ties to their home country. Immigrants today frequently travel back and forth to visit family and communicate regularly with them, in addition to sending money and goods to their families abroad. Many immigrants migrate back to their home country seasonally or do not permanently settle in the U.S., returning, for example, after retiring or when unable to find steady work or make sufficient money to support a life in the U.S., as has been observed with the global and US financial crisis of 2007-2010 and subsequent recession. This has given rise to transnational immigrant communities, a defining characteristic of immigrants in the U.S. today compared to immigrants who arrived earlier, particularly during the large waves of European immigration at the turn of the twentieth century, who permanently settled in the U.S. and separated from their home country. This characteristic is evident among the Dominican demographic today. Because the Dominican Republic is so close to the U.S. and travel between the island and the U.S. eastern seaboard relatively easy, there is a steady movement of people, a circular migration pattern, back and forth. Thus, there is a steady bi-directional flow of people, goods, and ideas, between the U.S. and the island (Bailey, 2000; Bailey, 2002). This has fostered the development of a bi-national Dominican community, as their lives span both countries, which has distinct implications. In particular, although the concept of family is in large part defined by co-habitation, Dominican families are often split between the island and the U.S. for some time (Bailey, 2000). This might help to explain why Dominicans have lower marriage rates compared to Latinos overall, and the higher rate of single-mother headed households observed among Caribbean immigrants compared to other urban immigrant groups (Kasinitz, et al., 2008).

Providence, RI and the Providence Latino and Dominican Communities

Providence, RI was one of the first cities established in the colonies, before the inception of this country, and is one of the largest cities in New England. It has a history of immigration, and immigrants from the late 1800s through early 1900s largely fostered its growth and prosperity. However, as a former manufacturing town, Providence has suffered extensively from the loss of manufacturing, as has the state of RI overall and other New England cities. Similar to many post-industrial cities throughout New England, poverty is a persistent problem. In 2006-2008, 20.5 percent of families and 26 percent of individuals were below the poverty line, compared to 9.6 percent and 13.2 of the total US population, respectively, as were 36.3 percent of all children under eighteen. Along various measures, income in

Providence was far below that of the whole country. Median household income ($36,298) was $15,877 less, median family income ($43,477) $19,734 less, and per capita income ($21,108) $6,358 less compared to national averages. By all indicators, Providence has a poverty problem which has certainly only been exacerbated by the economic crisis of 2007-2010 and high unemployment in RI, which according to the US Department of Labor, Bureau of Labor Statistics was 12.3 percent in May of 2010 compared to a national average of 9.7 percent. The unemployment rate in Providence was slightly elevated at 12.5 percent for the Providence-Fall River-Warwick, RI-MA Metropolitan area.

Providence has a large Latino community comprised of people with Caribbean, Mexican, Central American, and South American origins. According to the 2006-2008 ACS, 37.6 percent of the population of Providence was Latino, a seven percent increase from 2000. Dominicans are the largest Latino national group in the city. Of 63,778 persons of Latino ethnicity 23,533 were Dominican, up from 14,638 in 2000. Puerto Ricans (15,455) are the second largest group, followed by Guatemalans (11,385) and Mexicans (2,353). Although New York City is the primary Dominican enclave in the U.S., Providence can be considered a "secondary" enclave (Funkhouser and Ramos 1993). Dominicans in Providence are part of a larger, well established and strongly interconnected pan-ethnic Latino community. Although Latinos have roots in diverse countries, they share a common language, Spanish, a history of Spanish conquest and colonization, and Catholicism, which is the dominant religion throughout Latin America and is a defining characteristic of Latinos in the U.S. They also all hail from countries with lengthy histories of U.S. political, military, and economic intervention that reflects U.S domination in the western hemisphere as codified in the Monroe Doctrine (Peréa & García Coll, 2008). The Providence Latino community has a strong and vivacious small-business presence, cultural organizations and resources such as those afforded through the church, media, and community groups, as well as a very strong web of social networks. It is a dynamic and vivacious community that reflects its diversity, and has more Latin American and Spanish language cultural resources than it would have if it were solely comprised of Dominicans (Bailey, 2000, 2002).

An estimated 29.4 percent of the population of Providence was foreign born in 2006-2008, which increased from 25.3 percent in 2000, far greater than the 12.5 percent of the total U.S. population. The large immigrant population translates into a large number of people who speak a language other than English, which has been steadily growing along with an increase in the foreign-born population over the last decade. Close to half (47.8%) of the population age five and older spoke a language other than English at home in 2006-2008, an increase from 43 percent in 2000, compared to 19.6 percent of the total US population in 2000 and 17.9 percent in 2006-2008. Of the 75,348 people who reported speaking a language other than English at home, the vast majority, 54,867, spoke Spanish, of whom 27.2 % were age 5-17, 68.4 percent ages 18-64, and 4.4 percent over 65. Among people who spoke Spanish at home, the majority (56%) were foreign born, of whom 41.1 percent were naturalized US citizens. Poverty was higher among people who spoke Spanish, 30.1 percent compared to 21.9 percent among those who only spoke English. Seventy percent of Spanish speakers were at or above poverty compared to 78.1 percent of people who only spoke English. Among Latinos, more than half of the demographic, 25,250 of 52,146, were foreign-born in 2000, and the vast majority, 42,310, spoke Spanish. Among the 14,638 people of Dominican origin in Providence in 2000, 10,607 were foreign born, almost all of whom, 13,169, spoke Spanish. These characteristics illustrate that Providence is very much an immigrant city.

The high rate of poverty among Spanish speakers reflects the poverty status of Latinos in Providence overall. Thirty percent of Latino families and 32 percent of Latino individuals were below poverty in 2006-2008. However, the poverty rate among single-female headed Latina households was more than 3.5 times greater than the rate among married-couple Latino families, 52.6 percent compared to 14.1 percent, respectively. The economic characteristics of Dominicans in Providence are particularly abysmal. In 2000, median household income was $19,590, median family income $18,980, and per capita income $8,844, all far below the aforementioned state and national averages. Of the 14,638 Dominicans in Providence in 2000, 6,069 individuals were below poverty, as were 1,668 families. The high rates of poverty among Latinos in Providence, the majority of whom are Dominican, reflect low levels of educational attainment. Forty-five percent of Spanish speakers age twenty-five and older had less than a high school education, 28.5 percent had graduated high school, and only 10.8 percent had earned a Bachelor's degree or higher. Of the 7,964 Dominicans age 25 and older in 2000, only 557 had earned a Bachelor's degree or higher, and 3,667 had at least a high school diploma.

Growth among the immigrant child population is having a particular impact on the Providence schools, as is the case in schools across the country. As indicated in Table 1 below, demographic shifts and high poverty rates are evident in the large number of Latino, limited English proficient and poor students (as measured by qualification for free or reduced price lunch).

Table 1: Providence School Demographics, School Year 2009-2010, by grade level (percentages)

Group	Grade												
	1	2	3	4	5	6	7	8	9	10	11	12	Average
Latino	58	60	63	63	61	61	60	62	61	58	58	55	60
English Language Learner/ Limited English Proficient	24	24	24	17	15	9	8	9	10	10	8	6	15
Free or Reduced Price Lunch	88	88	93	91	90	89	88	86	85	83	82	78	87

Although Latinos in Providence comprise 37.6 percent of the population, among children under the age of 5 Latino children were 6,038 out of 12,607 in 2000- almost half of that demographic, illustrating the youthfulness of the population. Although not reflected in the above figures, this trend helps to understand the current composition of the Providence schools.

Discussion

The Dominican community in Providence is the result of increased migration from the Dominican Republic to the U.S., primarily over the last 20 years. The rate of immigration is high and steady to the point that Dominicans are now the fifth largest Latino national group in the U.S. Providence is an immigrant city that has a large, young, and growing Dominican community. At the same time it is a poor and high-poverty demographic with relatively low levels of educational attainment. These poor indicators shape the lives of Dominican children, and illustrate the resources and vulnerabilities that characterize their life circumstances.

The demographic profile of Dominicans illustrates the confluence of low socioeconomic status, language, immigrant status, race/ethnicity, and gender. It is reasonable to propose that these contextual factors impact the growth and development of Dominican children and youth, shaping their trajectories and futures. Because Dominican children comprise such a large and growing segment of the Latino demographic, particularly in Providence, understanding how they are doing along a variety of measures is important for understanding how they are faring in our society and what their trajectories are. It is important to understand the factors that put Dominican children on pathways to more optimal outcomes. It is also important to identify the characteristics of, and means by which to create enabling environments for Dominican children that foster optimal growth and development, as well as to address, if not avoid entirely, the factors that put this population of children at risk. Because performance in school is one of the key developmental tasks of childhood, and moreover because educational attainment is a key predictor of upward mobility, socioeconomic status and health in adulthood and throughout life, understanding how Dominican children are performing in school is important for understanding their current state and future trajectories. Understanding their individual trajectories will help to gauge where the population is headed as a whole, and will help us take steps to put Dominican children on positive pathways to achievement, health, fulfillment and success in life, as opposed to pathways to disparities.

CHAPTER 3

What do we know about Children of Immigrant Families?

High rates of immigration and the parallel growth of the Latino demographic are having a dramatic effect on the United States. Because of this current trend, children of immigrant families have become the fastest growing segment of the U.S. child population. Consequently, the number of Latino and Spanish speaking language minority children in U.S. schools has increased dramatically and continues to rise.

The successful incorporation of immigrants is critical for the entire nation, and thus dependent upon the academic success of their children. It has been well documented that education is strongly positively correlated with a variety of socioeconomic, health and behavioral outcomes. Thus, the academic success of children of immigrants is a key policy issue, as how they perform in school is arguably a determinant of how this demographic will fair in our society. Furthermore, research suggests a link between academic outcomes and acculturation. Thus, it is important to understand what effects, if any, adjusting to life in the U.S. has on academic performance for children of immigrant families, and what factors impact educational achievement. Additionally, differences in academic performance between girls/women and men/boys have been well documented, and studies have found difference in the achievement and pathways of immigrant children along gender lines. Thus, it is equally important to examine how gender shapes or determines performance in school for immigrant children. This chapter will review the relevant literature on acculturation, gender, and the education of children of immigrant families in the U.S. It will close with a discussion of the limitations of existing research.

The Life Circumstances of Children of Immigrant

Children of immigrant families contend with a variety of challenges that may hinder their ability to do well in school (Kao, 1999). Specifically, they face certain problems that native-born children do not, such as learning a language- English- that their parents likely do not speak at home. Children of immigrant families are also more likely to be poor: in 2003, 54 percent of children of immigrants lived in families with incomes below 200 percent of poverty, compared to 36 percent of children of non-immigrant families (Capps, et al., 2005). They are more than two times as likely to lack health insurance (Capps, et al., 2005, Shields, & Behrman, 2004), not to visit a health care provider on a regular basis (Brown et. al, 1999), and four times as likely to live in crowded housing (Shields, & Behrman, 2004). They are also less likely to be in center-based child care, which may limit their preparedness for formal schooling (Capps, et al., 2005).

In addition, children of immigrants tend to come from large families and have many siblings. Their parents generally have a low level of education and little knowledge of English, tend to be low-skilled and work in low-wage jobs, and have little understanding of and familiarity with this country's most basic institutions, such as schools (Hernandez and Darke, 1999). Particular to children of immigrant children is the issue of status, particularly of their parents. Many have parents who are undocumented which may subject them to certain hardships (Capps, et al., 2005). In their research of over 400 adolescents of immigrant families in NYC, including children with families from the Dominican Republic, Suarez-Orozco, Suarez-Orozco & Todorova (2008) found that more than three quarters had endured a period of separation from one or both of their parents ranging from six months to as much as ten years. They found that the longer children were separated from their parents, the more children reported symptoms of anxiety and depression. Growing up in such uncertainty poses significant developmental implications and underscores their unique mental health needs (Suarez-Orozco, 2010). One can only wonder how this affects their sense of being able to participate in our society, or sense of empowerment by participating in our institutions, such as our schools, in the country in which the majority of immigrant children are born and raised, the only country many of them have ever known.

Although most immigrant parents place tremendous value on education and have high hopes and expectations for their children, immigrant parents often are not very involved in their children's education. Because of their lack of familiarity with the school system, immigrant parents frequently do not know what they can do to foster their children's success in school (García Coll, et al., 2002). In addition, many do not believe that parents should be involved in education, and thus do not participate in the typical parent involvement activities of white middle class families (Delgado-Gaitan, 1992; Okagaki, 2001; Suarez-Orozco & Suarez-Orozco, 2001; Valdés, 1996). The challenges children of immigrant families face are exacerbated by the fact that they often lack adequate English language skills themselves and, because they tend to live in poor urban neighborhoods, attend large, segregated, inner-city schools with few well qualified and certified teachers, overcrowded classrooms, dilapidated facilities, and outdated curricula, where parent involvement is not just not encouraged but often explicitly discouraged (Nord & Griffin, 1999, Ruiz-de-Velasco & Fix 2000). Furthermore, Limited English Proficient (LEP) children (primarily immigrants themselves or born in the US to immigrant parents) are a largely segregated subpopulation- almost 70 percent of LEP students are enrolled in only 10 percent of US schools (Cosentino de Cohen, Deterding, & Clewell, 2005).

These realities pose certain liabilities for children and their development. Specifically, low levels of academic achievement are associated with many of the challenges children of immigrants face: poverty, low socioeconomic status, low levels of maternal education, and minority status (Alexander, Entwisle & Kabbani, 2001; Duncan & Brooks-Gunn, 2000; Gringlas & Weinraub, 1995; McLanahan & Sandefur, 1994; McLoyd, 1998). Although some research has found that not all children with such risk factors have low levels of academic achievement (Finn & Rock, 1997), children of immigrants face obstacles to educational success.

Acculturation

In spite of the many risks they face, studies have found that children of immigrants are doing fairly well in school. However, the research has found a negative association between acculturation and academic performance, as well as other health and behavioral outcomes.

According to Berry (Berry, et al., 1992), acculturation is a process that unfolds from contact between groups, and characterizes how a person responds to and orients him or herself to a changing cultural context. Acculturation is a process that results in certain socio-cultural adaptations, or the long term ways in which a person rearranges her/his life, and how well s/he can settle-down and manage day to day life in their new cultural context (Berry, et al., 1992, p.369-370). There are different acculturation types, for example, a person can assimilate, relinquish or not acquire the cultural practices, language, and behaviors of their country/family, or they can become bicultural, maintaining the language and culture of their family/country while learning the culture and language of the culture they are becoming part of. Sometimes, if acculturation is thought of as a linear process, "degree" of acculturation (i.e., "greater" or "more" acculturation") is used to denote acculturation type, as an indicator of how "American" a person is, defined as how far removed they are from the culture of their country of origin. (For a more detailed discussion of this see Chapter 4, Theoretical Frameworks.) It is through the process of acculturation that immigrants adapt to life in a new country that is culturally dissimilar from where they or their families came.

Contrary to prevailing ideas of immigrant incorporation and traditional theories of assimilation, the studies reviewed in the following pages have found that, for some immigrant populations, those who are less acculturated often have more favorable educational outcomes than those who are more acculturated, and compared to native-born individuals of the same ethnic or national group as well as the white majority population. The research has also found a positive association between bilingualism and more positive academic, health and behavioral outcomes, indicating that bilingual/bicultural children are healthier, do better in school, and engage in fewer risky behaviors. This suggests that bilingualism/biculturalism functions as a protective factor that can offset some of the vulnerabilities immigrant children face, mitigate their negative effects, and shelter children against academic failure, such as doing poorly in or dropping out of school, by providing them with tools that help them do better academically. However, there are differences among and within groups, and the processes/mechanisms through which these things unfold are not well understood.

Language, Acculturation, and Academic Performance

There is relatively little research on how immigrant children fare in school, particularly the second generation. In an early study, Suarez-Orozco and Suarez-Orozco (1995) examined school attitudes among a diverse sample of Mexican origin adolescents (first generation Mexican immigrant, second generation Mexican-American1) and white students. The study found some early indications that acculturation was associated with attitudes towards school, specifically that less acculturation is associated with more positive attitudes, which the research suggests are the foundation of future academic performance. They found that white students knew they had to do well in school in order to have a fulfilling and stable future. However, compared to Mexican-origin students, they were more likely to be angry and frustrated about school, and displayed a high degree of ambivalence towards school and especially school authority figures. Mexican immigrant students had comparatively more positive attitudes towards school and school authorities than white students. They were also more appreciative of their opportunity for an education, believed school authority figures were fair and had respect for them, and expressed feelings of sadness and shame when they were disciplined because they felt they were letting their teachers down. Among first generation Mexican students, they found that students who were less acculturated-those who maintained more of the home culture and language- had a more positive attitude toward school and had higher educational expectations than their Mexican peers of the same generation who were more acculturated. As a group, some second generation Mexican-American students had the same attitudes as first generation Mexican immigrant students, whereas some had attitudes towards school like those of white students. The researchers suggested that this indicates a blend of attitudes reflective of their higher level of acculturation compared to the less acculturated first generation students, but that they are also not as acculturated as the white students.

In their longitudinal study of high school students, Kao & Tienda (1995) studied the relationship between generational status and academic performance among immigrant students. Using a nationally representative sample of 24,599 students in 1,052 randomly selected schools, they followed students from the eighth through twelfth grade to understand educational achievement (grades, test scores, college aspirations) and assess if it was associated with generational status and length of residency, which are proxies for acculturation. Their research found that students' generational status had important consequences for academic performance. They also found that racial/ethnic differences in academic performance were relatively absent among the first generation, but became more important as length of residency increased with subsequent generations. Interestingly, they found that parents' immigrant status had more of an influence on academic performance than the generational status of the child, although generational status could explain more of the variation in educational outcomes among Asian students than among white students or students of other minority groups. Although they found little difference in academic performance between first and second generation immigrant students, first and second generation students outperformed students of the third or higher generation. In other words, students who themselves or their families had been in the U.S. for shorter periods of time did better in school than those who had been here longer.

Suarez-Orozco and Suarez-Orozco (1995) findings were supported by Rumbaut's (1995) comparative study of students in the San Diego, California schools, which also found evidence of a negative association between greater acculturation (as measured by language) and academic performance. The study compared the academic performance of students of various national immigrant groups and white students, and specifically examined the impact of language, namely English language proficiency, on academic outcomes. The study collected data on almost 80,000 high school students in their sophomore, junior and senior year in two cohorts during the 1986-1987 and 1989-1990 school years. More than a third of the sample was Latino, primarily of Mexican-origin (20%), and approximately 17 percent were Asian. Among Latino and Asian students 75 percent spoke a language other than English at home. The San Diego school district used an English language proficiency assessment tool to classify students as Limited English Proficient (LEP) or Fluent English Proficient (FEP). Rumbaut (1995) treated these classifications like the measures of bilingualism proposed by Peal and Lambert (1962), where FEP was equated with being a "balanced bilingual", defined as someone who can effectively and competently communicate in two languages, and LEP was equated with being a "semi-bilingual," defined as someone who knows one language much better than the other and who does not communicate in the second language (Portes & Rumbaut, 2006). These classifications were used to test for correlations between English language proficiency and various measures of academic performance (grade point average, standardized test scores and drop-out rates).

During the years of the study, the average grade point average (GPA) for all students was 2.11, and for white students it was 2.24. However, both averages were surpassed by the GPAs of all Asian national groups in the study (Chinese students surpassed the average GPA by one full point). Importantly, they found that FEP students (also defined as fluent bilinguals in this study) did better than LEP and English monolingual students of the same ethnic group, as well as better than white majority students.

On tests of reading comprehension, English monolinguals tended to have the highest test scores, with white majority students performing the best. As stated by Portes and Rumbaut (2006), "this result essentially confirms the validity of the linguistic classification of students by saying that those who are supposed to know English best actually do" (p.215). However, on standardized math tests FEP or fluent bilingual students had significantly higher scores than white majority, English monolingual, and lower performing bilingual students, for every national group in the study.

This study did not have a selection bias favoring students who remained in school (non- drop-outs), rather it included students who either dropped-out or left the district. Analyses of drop out rates in the San Diego school district for the 1989-1990 cohort found that Chinese language minority students had the lowest drop out rate. Furthermore, LEP students in every immigrant national group had a significantly higher drop-out risk than FEP students. Among Asian students, FEP students had significantly lower drop out rates than English monolinguals.

Although there were important differences among groups in Rumbaut's (1995) work, being bilingual emerged as a protective factor. The study's findings about language and academic performance support the idea that greater bilingualism (as opposed to limited bilingualism or English monolingualism) is an asset that can function as a protective factor for children of immigrant families- and that more acculturation (loss of the home culture and language) can be a liability for immigrant children. As Rumbaut points out, this result provides support for the concept of "additive" rather than "subtractive" acculturation (p. 52), denoting when a cultural/linguistic resource is either maintained or lost, respectively, through the process of acculturation. The findings from Rumbaut also support the findings by Peal and Lambert (1992) in their study of French monolingual and English-French bilingual children in Montreal. In their influential and carefully controlled study of French monolinguals and balanced French-English bilingual ten-year-olds, they found that, when controlling for demographic factors and socioeconomic status, bilingual students performed significantly better than monolingual children on a battery of both verbal and non-verbal IQ tests. This little known research contradicted decades of heavily biased and methodologically unsound research on bilingualism (Peréa & García Coll, 2008; Portes & Rumbaut, 2006; Suarez-Orozco & Suarez-Orozco, 2001).

Fuligni (1997) studied 1,100 sixth, eighth, and tenth graders of Latino, East Asian, Filipino, and European descent, focusing on the impact of family background, parent attitudes towards schooling, peer support, and adolescents' attitudes and behaviors towards school and academic performance. The study found that first and second generation immigrant students out performed third generation immigrant students in math and English. These successes were achieved even though they were more likely to come from families where English was not the primary language. Although socioeconomic status was associated with performance in English and math, only a small portion of academic success was attributable to socioeconomic status. A more significant correlate was a strong emphasis on education that was shared by students, parents, and peers, although parent education and occupation accounted for only a small portion of children's academic success. Ethnic background was also associated with academic performance: East Asian students had the highest grades and Latino students had the lowest. However, when controlling for ethnicity, foreign-born students performed significantly better than their third generation peers in both math and English. In addition, when controlling for ethnic background, Fuligni found that generational status was negatively related to academic motivation, and that compared to their third generation peers, first generation children placed a higher value on their education, had higher educational aspirations and expectations, and reported feeling higher expectations and aspirations from their parents. Lastly, the girls from immigrant families tended to have higher grades in math and English courses than the boys.

The study findings are contrary to theories that low socioeconomic status places students at greater risk for doing poorly in school. Portes and MacLeod (1999), expanded on existing research by looking closely at how parents' socioeconomic status, human capital factors and modes of immigrant incorporation influence academic achievement among second generation immigrant students. They found that, after controlling for parental education, language, skills (human capital), and family structure (social networks), differences in academic achievement across students of different national groups disappeared. However, after controlling for group differences in the context of reception and immigration history, differences in academic performance among children of different national groups were evident. Results indicated that socioeconomic status could only partially predict academic performance, in which case children of immigrants are no different from peers with US-born parents.

The Children of Immigrants Longitudinal Study (CILS) is the largest study of immigrant children to date, specifically second generation immigrant youth. The CILS sampled over 5,000 children and their families, and was based primarily on a series of surveys with children and their immigrant parents between 1992 and 1996. The CILS looked at diverse national groups, and focused on second generation children of immigrants from Cuba, Nicaragua, Haiti, the Dominican Republic, Trinidad, Mexico, Vietnam, the Philippines, Cambodia, and Laos. This is different from many earlier studies which had looked at only a handful of pan-ethnic groups, such as "Latino" and "Asian," as opposed to distinct national groups. The study is the most comprehensive study of the immigrant second generation to date, and attempted to cover numerous intertwined issues. Portes and Rumbaut (2001) used the CILS for a longitudinal study of second generation immigrant teens in the Miami and San Diego metro areas. They sought to understand the collective influence of immigrant incorporation, immigrant status, parent education, socioeconomic status, and of multiple contexts (the home/family, school, community) on academic outcomes. One of the many strengths of this research is that it was designed to look at different national groups comparatively, for example, how Vietnamese and Cuban students fair in Miami compared to each other, as well as individually in order to understand the observed academic outcomes relative to the particular realities and unique characteristics of each group. Their study's underlying theory is segmented assimilation and acculturation, a theory that proposes there is not one, but various immigrant experience and outcomes that depend on where immigrants come from and how they are received in this country (Portes and Rumbaut, 2001, Portes and Zhou, 1993). Segmented assimilation and acculturation is based on the understanding that acculturation is not a uniform or linear process, and that immigrants and their children adjust to life in the US using different strategies and following different paths. As Portes & Rumbaut (2001) state, "the process [of acculturation] is subject to too many contingencies and affected by too many variables to render the image of a relatively uniform and straightforward path credible. Instead, the present second generation is better defined as undergoing a process of segmented assimilation where outcomes vary across immigrant minorities and where rapid integration and acceptance into the American mainstream represent just one possible solution" (p.45).

Many interesting findings emerged from the CILS, one being that children who had been in this country for a longer period of time were less motivated towards school. With regard to language, they found substantial evidence that greater acculturation is associated with poorer academic outcomes, specifically that bilingualism functioned as a protective factor for children from immigrant families. The research found that loss of the home/family language was strongly associated with cultural dissonance, namely increased parent-child conflict, which was found to have a consistently strong, negative effect on academic achievement. The data also showed that although children of immigrant families were doing fairly well in school and that greater acculturation led to greater English language proficiency- usually an unquestioned good thing- it also led to less effort in school and lower grades. The authors propose that as second generation children increasingly acculturate to U.S. culture, losing the home/family language and culture, they gradually lose their drive to achieve in school, resulting in lower grades.

Portes and Rumbaut (2001) found that increased length of residency and acculturation type (assimilated/English only; bilingual/bicultural) profoundly influence children's academic performance. They offer an alternative to prevailing strategies of forceful assimilation, such as English immersion, which they call "selective acculturation." Selective acculturation entails the exact opposite of assimilation as an acculturation strategy, namely maintenance of the home culture and language, while learning English and the dominant American culture. In essence, Portes and Rumbaut suggest that biculturalism/bilingualism is an appropriate acculturation strategy for second generation children of immigrant families. They make this recommendation based on the many benefits of preservation of the home/family language and culture they found in their research, and the liabilities associated with assimilation and loss of the home/family language and culture. Specifically, they found that selective acculturation, which is intertwined with fluent bilingualism, is associated with higher academic and occupational aspirations and expectations, better academic outcomes, greater self-esteem, and less parent-child conflict.

In a supplement to CILS study findings in 2001, Portes and Hao (2004) analyzed the school contextual effects of the CILS data. Using a hierarchical model of contextual and individual level effects on academic achievement and school attrition, they studied 5,266 second generation children who were originally interviewed during the 1992–1993 school year when they were in the 8th and 9th grades. Consistent with earlier studies of the CILS and other research, the study found that longer periods of US residency had a negative effect on academic performance regardless of school context. Although this research did not examine language specifically, the findings are consistent with previous studies of the effects of greater acculturation. As the researchers posit, "this result points to the influence of acculturation in bringing down the initial achievement drive among immigrant youths to the level predominant among native-parentage students" (p.11926).

To better understand variations in educational attainment among young adults of various backgrounds, Rumbaut (2008) used data samples from the third wave of the CILS and the study of Immigration and Intergenerational Mobility in Metropolitan Los Angeles (IIMMLA), to examine the educational mobility of 1.5 (foreign-born, arriving when 0-12 years of age) and second-generation young adults of Mexican, Salvadoran, Guatemalan, Filipino, Chinese, Korean, Vietnamese, Cambodian, and Laotian descent. The study found that young adults with foreign–born parents are demonstrating educational progress, but at different rates depending on class, ethnicity, and gender. There was no overarching trend or single mobility trajectory found across all ethnic groups to emerge from this research. The Chinese and Koreans have made exceptional academic achievements in both high school scores and rates of postsecondary matriculation and graduation. Filipinos have a moderate level of achievement above that of white majority students. However, 1.5 generation Mexicans are twice as likely to drop out of high school as graduate from college. Salvadorans, Guatemalans, Cambodians, and Laotians were in the middle, with slightly less high school dropouts than college graduates. Study results point to the influence of various contextual factors and individual characteristics on educational outcomes, as well as the interactions among them, illustrating the non-uniform or linear nature of acculturation and adjustment.

Using 1990 Census data, Feliciano (2001) examined language use, the language spoken in the home, the presence of immigrants in the household, and school drop-out rates among Vietnamese, Korean, Mexican, Puerto Rican, Cuban, Chinese, Filipino, and Japanese youths age 18-21 to determine if maintenance of the parents' immigrant culture was beneficial or detrimental to academic attainment (a white comparison group was included as well). The study's key finding was that bilingualism/biculturalism as well as exposure to the parents' immigrant culture did not increase the probability that youth in any of the immigrant groups would drop out of school. The study found that the effect of language and the proportion of foreign born persons in the home were all significant predictors of academic attainment when controlling for sex, age, and socioeconomic status.

Overall, youths living in homes where everyone was an immigrant were about half as likely to drop out as those in households where everyone was born in the US. Most importantly, youth who spoke English only were 43 percent more likely to drop out than bilinguals, and those in homes where everyone was bilingual were half as likely to drop out of school compared to youth living in homes with no bilingual persons. Similar to previous studies, the results indicate that youth who have acculturated while maintaining ties to the home language and culture, those who speak English very well but live in bilingual immigrant households, are the least likely to drop out of school. These findings suggest that those youth who can have tap into both the mainstream and home culture are the most successful academically.

To better understand the possible effects of pre-migration family characteristics, and factors in the home country on educational attainment among second generation immigrant students in the US, Feliciano (2006) examined educational selectivity, defined as the difference between immigrants' educational attainment and the average educational attainment in their homeland. Underscoring the need to understand contextual factors in the sending country, not just in the US, the receiving country, as well as the assets and vulnerabilities immigrants possess, Feliciano emphasized the importance of understanding immigrants' economic and educational status prior to migration to help determine where their children will end up in the class and educational stratification system in the US. To this end, educational selectivity provides a more adequate assessment of the roots of educational attainment because it captures skill level and relative pre-migration status instead of only considering the immigrants' status once they have come to the US.

The study consisted of analyses of data from published educational attainment statistics in thirty-two of the top-immigrant-sending countries to the US, as well as US census data on immigrants from those countries. To examine effects on the second generation, she merged data from the CILS (Portes & Rumbaut, 2001) with US Census data on adult immigrants from the 19 countries whose second generation children were represented in the CILS data. With this sample, she sought to explain ethnic group differences in educational outcomes and to shed light on why some immigrants and their children are more successful in the US than others.

Among the most important findings from this research, the study revealed that, although there is substantial variation, nearly all US immigrants are positively selected, specifically that they are more educated than the populations in their home countries. This finding carries profound implications for immigrants' adjustment to US society. Firstly, immigrants from highly selective groups have higher aspirations, leading to greater educational expectations and aspirations among their children. Even if an individual immigrant's economic situation is poor, the child's aspirations will still be high because of the overriding influence of group-level factors on the second generation's educational aspirations and, consequently, attainment. Feliciano also found that as the relative level of education attained by immigrants in their home countries increases, the educational attainment of their second generation children increases as well. The study also found that the acculturation and mobility patterns of US immigrants are dependent on pre-migration socioeconomic status and educational attainment. Immigrants who had a high status in their home country were found to have significant upward mobility in the new country, illustrating that immigrants' pre-migration socioeconomic status is a more accurate marker of assimilation patterns than post-migration socioeconomic status. The implications of these findings indicate that immigrants' educational attainment and socioeconomic status in their home country are major determinants of their children's educational attainment and socioeconomic status in the adopted country. In conclusion Feliciano proposes that education serves to reproduce the family's social location in the home country in the US, and does not necessarily lend itself to upward mobility.

Substantial evidence nevertheless points to a negative effect of increased length of residency on academic performance, as evident from a recent study which found differences among children with foreign born and US-born parents. Using data from the National Longitudinal Study of Adolescent Health, Pong and Hao (2007) examined neighborhood and school level effects on achievement among adolescent youth from immigrant families of different ethnicities and nativities. In a study of 17,262 youth in 127 schools in grades 7 and 8, of whom 4,271 were children of immigrants, researchers studied 1600 Latino and 792 Asian youth of diverse ethnic groups (Mexican, Puerto Rican, Cuban, Chinese and Filipino), in the first, second, and pre-school generations (the preschool generation was defined as those who immigrated to the US before the age of six), in addition to non-Hispanic whites and blacks. Using hierarchical models, results indicated that the overall socioeconomic status of the neighborhood had a positive effect on GPA, however further analysis revealed that the association existed among immigrants' children, but not among the children of US born parents. Family socioeconomic status was found to be highly predictive of GPA among the children of US born parents, as well as among immigrants' children, although to a lesser degree. Overall, the first and preschool generations were found to have a higher GPA than second generation children. Differences in family background, as well as neighborhood and school conditions did not explain the advantage of foreign birth. Second generation Latinos were found to have far lower GPAs than non-Hispanic whites, whereas second generation Chinese were found to have higher grades than non-Hispanic whites. Furthermore, second generation children who did not speak English or Spanish at home, so those who spoke native Chinese and Filipino languages had superior performance compared to their English speaking peers. However, speaking Spanish was related to lower GPA in children of immigrants but not among children of natives.

The Pong and Hao (2007) study show that there are generational differences among and within diverse pan-ethnic groups in this country, which are associated with academic performance. Furthermore, the results indicate that the effects of Spanish language usage on academic performance differ depending on generational status among Latino adolescents. The study raises important questions, and points to the importance of examining contexts beyond the family in order to understand key outcomes such as academic performance. Importantly, the study demonstrates the need for within group studies of children of different generations to better understand how these dynamics might unfold over time as children grow up and with greater length of residency in this country.

Although most studies to date have found a positive association between bilingualism/biculturalism and academic performance, and a negative association between greater acculturation (assimilation)/ speaking English only and performance in school, some studies have had mixed results. In their study of sixty ninth grade Mexican origin students in the three high schools in a southwestern US school district, Lopez et al. (2002) examined the impact of acculturation and social support on academic achievement, as measured by grade point average (GPA). Only students who identified as Mexican origin were included in the study. Although the study found that the degree of acculturation was not associated with academic performance, the results indicated that the type of acculturation (e.g., bicultural, assimilated) was significantly related to achievement. The researchers hypothesized that this mixed finding might have resulted from the use of poor measures, specifically that the measures used were not fine enough to capture the variability within degree of acculturation, and that a more comprehensive and inclusive measure of acculturation that accounted for variations in cultural norms and values might be needed. In sum, the results indicated that bicultural students tended to have higher levels of academic achievement. This is consistent with previous studies as the results indicate that youth who perform better in school are those who adopt the behaviors and values of the dominant culture needed in school while maintaining the home/family culture and language. Girls were found to have higher GPAs although they were less acculturated than the boys, who were slightly more acculturated and had lower grades, suggesting an interaction between gender and acculturation.

Many studies have focused on the immigrant second generation. However, in one of the largest and most distinct studies to date, the Longitudinal Immigrant Student Adaptation Study (LISA), Suarez-Orozco, Suarez-Orozco & Todorova (2008) conducted a five year longitudinal study of newly arrived first generation immigrant youth seeking to explain differences in academic performance. Starting with a sample of 407 in year one and closing with a sample of 309 in year five (less than 5% annual attrition), the study examined the experiences of immigrant students, including the impact of learning English, language comfort and proficiency on academic grades, among youth ages 9-14 from the Dominican Republic, Mexico, Central America, Haiti, and China attending public high schools in the Boston and San Francisco areas. Participants had been in the U.S. an average of five years. all spoke a language other than English, and parents interviewed as part of the study all chose to speak in their native language

The study found that immigrant youth express tremendous hope and optimism about their opportunities and futures when they come to the U.S, and are excited about education and the possibilities it presents. However, because they overwhelmingly live in poor urban communities and are subjected to inadequate, segregated, high-poverty schools, they lose the hope, optimism and enthusiasm they came with. Furthermore, although they might learn English, they fail to learn the academic English they need to succeed in school and beyond. Results indicated that the GPAs of all students dropped over the five years of the study. However, they found that students who were successful had supportive and encouraging relationships with parents, teachers, and mentors, whereas those who didn't tended to become increasingly frustrated and disengaged from school. By grouping the students into five pathways of academic performance, high performers, slow decliners, precipitous decliners, improvers, and low achievers, the researchers found that improvers were more likely to be girls who had a supportive relationship with an adult or mentor.

A key component of the study examined the impact of English and native language proficiency on academic grades and achievement test scores. The study also sought to determine whether students were learning the academic English they need to compete and succeed in school and beyond. The Bilingual Verbal Abilities Test2 (BVAT) was administered to assess language proficiency and academic preparedness in years three and five. The test yields an English language proficiency (ELP) score and a Gain score that captures academic conceptual knowledge and understanding and accounts for use of both English and the test takers use of her/his native language. The ELP and Gain scores are combined to produce a bilingual verbal ability (BVA) score.

In year five of the LISA study, only 7 percent of the sample had and ELP score at or above the mean (100) for native English speakers of the same age. The mean for students in the study was 74.7. Students in the study had scores equal to the lowest two percentiles of their native English speaking peers. Only 22 percent of students were within one standard deviation of the mean of native English speaking peers, and more than 75 percent were more than one standard deviation below that mean. Only 9.3 percent of Dominican youth in the sample had an ELP score of 85 or greater. There was a clear association between ELP scores and academic pathway group, as high achievers had a higher mean ELP score (91.3), whereas low achievers, precipitous decliners and improvers had scores that were more than two standard deviations below the mean. However, when students were able to use both English and their native language their Gain scores on average increased over one standard deviation, There was variation based on country of origin, as Chinese students were found to have significant higher cognitive academic skills compared to students from the other national origin groups. English proficiency scores increased at the same rate for students in each of the five pathways of academic performance.

However, the majority of students who had been in the US five years or more had academic English proficiency scores well behind their native English speaking peers. This finding supports research indicating that acquiring the language skills adequate for academic success take seven to ten years to acquire (Cummins, 1991). Although motivation is a significant predictor of performance in school, even students who were highly motivated struggled in more advanced courses in mainstream English-only programs with their U.S.-born peers.

Results indicated that the English language proficiency score on the BVAT was highly predictive of academic performance. Higher oral academic English was significantly correlated with higher grades as well as achievement test scores. However, it is important to note that indicators of school quality such as the segregation, poverty, and attendance rates, were all significantly correlated with students' English proficiency. This suggests that English language skills may be a proxy for, or may at least reflect, educational quality, which it is well documented is a significant predictor of academic outcomes. Succinctly stated, it may be that students in more optimal schools have higher grades than students in inadequate schools, or that students in more optimal schools are more likely to learn the English they need to have higher levels of academic performance, which might not be the case for students in poor quality schools. Furthermore, given the well established shortcomings of bilingual education programs and the schools that are attended by newly arrived immigrant students in general, the finding that students who have better English skills do better in school than those who do not may point to the inadequacy of such programs in preparing immigrant students to succeed academically in English language dominated and oriented schools and an overall majority school system.

The research on immigrants and acculturation to date has been primarily conducted with adolescents and adults. Moreover, studies of academic performance among immigrant children have focused exclusively on adolescents, and there is a dearth of research on pre-adolescent immigrant children in this area. Middle childhood is a historically understudied developmental period. However, it is a crucial stage in human development, as what happens during middle childhood can set children on certain trajectories shaping experiences and outcomes across the lifespan. In particular, some evidence suggests that academic performance in the elementary grades can predict academic performance in adolescence. Using data from the study Children of Immigrants: Development in Context, Peréa and colleagues (2006) found that elementary school GPA was highly predictive of academic outcomes in high school for Dominican and Cambodian adolescents, although there were differences between the two immigrant groups. In general, analyses showed that children who were doing well or excelling in elementary school were likely to be doing well in high school and children who were under-performing or at risk for academic failure in the upper elementary grades four to six were likely to be doing poorly in high school. Research has found that infancy and early childhood are critical periods in human development and what happens during that time can have huge and to some extent irreversible consequences for development, health and well being later in life (National Research Council and Institute of Medicine, 2000); and it is likely that what happens during middle childhood can have an equally profound impact. As Huston and Ripke (2006) argue: "although the preschool years establish the base for future development, experiences in middle childhood can sustain, magnify, or reverse the advantages or disadvantages that children acquire in the preschool years. At the same time, middle childhood is a pathway to adolescence, setting trajectories that are not easily changed later" (p. 2). Knowing and understanding what happens during childhood can perhaps shed light on adolescent phenomena as well as academic outcomes during youth.

The study Children of Immigrants: Development in Context (CIDC) (García Coll and Marks, 2009; García Coll, Szalacha, & Palacios, 2005; García Coll, et al., 2002) was the first study of its kind to examine immigrant children during middle childhood (roughly ages 6-12). In particular, it centered on questions about acculturation, language, culture, ethnicity, and their impact on academic outcomes. Data from the CIDC were used for the research presented in this text. The CIDC study (García Coll and Marks, 2009) was a two cohort, three year longitudinal study of children of immigrant families from the Dominican Republic, Cambodia, and Portugal living and attending schools in Providence and East Providence, RI. These three national groups represented the largest Latino, Asian and European ethnic groups in the Providence, RI metropolitan area. The purpose of the study was to (1) understand the psychosocial, emotional and academic development and orientation of immigrant children during middle childhood, and (2) learn how academic outcomes were impacted by the different contexts of development, such as family, community, and school. The study focused on (1) the development of ethnic/racial identity, (2) academic attitudes as function of family immigration history and adaptation, child and school characteristics, and (3) the relationship between ethnic identity development and school engagement. The study employed a mixed-methodology, and data were collected on the children, their parents/families, teachers, schools and communities through interviews, ethnography, academic records, school-level administrative records, observation and recording3.

Children were recruited from 26 public and 4 parochial schools with large numbers of Latino, Asian and White students. All children had at least one parent born in the Dominican Republic, Cambodia or Portugal. The sample consisted of 403 children (139 Dominican, 142 Cambodian, and 122 Portuguese). The younger age cohort (n=196, and median age 6.5) was in the first grade and the older age cohort (n= 207, and median age 9.4) in the fourth grade in year one of the study. There were 198 boys and 205 girls.

Findings from the CIDC illustrate the variation among diverse national origin groups. In terms of academic attitudes, Cambodian children had overall positive attitudes towards school and their teachers, although it was slightly less than that of either the Dominican or Portuguese children. As they became older, there was an improvement in their attitudes to more or less equal that of their peers from the other immigrant groups. However, results did not provide evidence of the immigrant paradox, as older children were found to have more positive attitudes, suggesting improvement over time (as opposed to the well documented deterioration) that may, in part, be a function of increased experience within U.S. schools.

Similar to the study by Suarez-Orozco, Suarez-Orozco & Todorova (2008), each child was placed into one of five pathways of academic performance: excelling, positive, mixed, negative or abysmal. These paths reflect a mixed qualitative and quantitative assessment and categorization of students' academic performance comprised of both academic grades and teacher reports. Among Cambodian children 56 percent were in either the excelling or positive pathway; 21 percent were categorized as excelling compared to only 10 percent of both

Dominican and Portuguese children. Cambodian children were also rated more highly by their teachers compared to children from the other immigrant groups.

Dominican children had relatively positive attitudes towards their teachers and had high levels of school engagement. More positive academic attitudes were found among the older cohort, suggesting they might improve with age among Dominican children. This is in contradiction with some of the research literature which has found a deterioration in academic attitudes over time. On average, Dominican students had a B average for academic grades and were rated relatively well by their teachers, however grades were higher among the younger children. Forty three percent of Dominican children were in either the excelling or positive pathways, which was equal to that of Portuguese children, but less than that of the Cambodian. Nevertheless, Dominican children were disproportionately in the lower achieving academic pathways, as a whopping 32 percent were in the abysmal or negative pathway compared to 20 percent of Cambodian children. Contrary to the immigrant paradox, the parents of children in the abysmal pathway were more likely to be recent arrivals compared to the parents of children in the excelling pathway,

Portuguese children were found to have generally positive academic attitudes much like their Dominican and Cambodian peers. These positive attitudes were also found to be higher among the older children, which is in contradiction to the immigrant paradox. Portuguese children also had significantly more positive perceptions of their teachers compared to children from the other two groups, and had higher levels of school engagement than their Cambodian peers. Similar to Cambodian and Dominican children, Portuguese children had a B average and grades were higher among the younger children. Teachers rated Portuguese children positively, for the most part, although girls more so than boys, but they were rated below Cambodian children. Their academic profile is similar to that of Dominican children, and fewer of them were in the excelling and positive pathways when compared to the Cambodian children.

Findings from the CIDC provide evidence of the various academic experiences and trajectories among elementary school age children of immigrant families. Although research has found deterioration in academic attitudes over time among native-born samples, this was not observed among any of the children in the CIDC study. To the contrary, results indicate a cohort effect whereby older children have more positive attitudes. If this is interpreted to mean that attitudes improve over time, the results provide evidence contrary to the immigrant paradox and in contradiction with much of the research literature (Alexander et al., 1997; Eccles, Midgley, & Adler, 1984). Although the Cambodian children had higher levels of achievement compared to children in either of the two other groups, most of the children (56% of Cambodians, and 44% of both Dominicans and Portuguese) had As and Bs as three-year GPAs. This would be consistent with previous research that has found immigrant children have higher levels of academic achievement compared to their U.S.-born peers (Fuligni, 1997; Kao & Tienda, 1995; Portes & Rumbaut, 2001).

Bilingual Education

There is growing evidence that maintenance of the home/family language may be an asset to children of immigrant families and may lead to higher levels of academic performance, findings that are supported by research in bilingual education. Research on bilingual education is conducted primarily to determine whether or not instruction in the native language facilitates English language learning and long-term academic achievement. One of the major problems with bilingual education research, however, is the number of diverse programs and practices that fall under the rubric of bilingual education. There are about as many successful programs as there are those that are riddled with various problems (National Research Council and Institute of Medicine, 1997). Although the evidence provides more support for bilingual education than it does against it, the research has not proved conclusively the superiority of bilingual education over monolingual English education for all children in all contexts (Crawford, 2000, p.84). Although research has not identified a single effective bilingual education program for English Language Learner (ELL) students, studies suggest there are perhaps various different methods and types of programs that are and would be successful in educating ELL students so they learn English and succeed academically.

What is clear, however, is that one-year of English instruction is generally insufficient to adequately prepare ELL students to succeed in

English-only classrooms (Ma, 2002; Suarez-Orozco & Suarez-Orozco, 2001). No study has found that English immersion is necessarily better, but various studies indicate that well-designed and implemented bilingual programs result in higher levels of academic achievement for ELL students, and that ELL students in these types of programs have test scores equal to or above those of their native English speaking peers (National Research Council and Institute of Medicine, 1997; Green, 1997; Ma, 2002; Thomas & Collier, 1997 and 2001; Willig 1985). Although Baker & de Kanter (1983) and Rossell & Baker (1996) sought to study transitional bilingual education (TBE) programs4, or compare TBE and English only or English immersion programs, these poorly designed studies were widely critiqued for having numerous flaws, primarily the inconsistent criteria used to select studies and its poor labeling of programs (Cummins, 1992; Stritikus, 2002; Stritikus & Manyak, 2000).

The research on second language acquisition suggests that the best predictor of English language achievement is skill in the first language, in that skills developed in the first language facilitate development of the second language (Thomas & Collier, 1997, 2001; Suarez-Orozco & Suarez-Orozco, 2001). In addition, use of a language other than English, either at home or at school, does not inhibit the development of English language skills. As August & Hakuta conclude in their review of bilingualism and second language learning sponsored by the National Research Council: "the use of a child's native language does not impede the acquisition of English," and effective schools for ELL students include "some use of the native language and culture in the instruction of language-minority students" (National Research Council and Institute of Medicine, 1997). In their review, they found that bilingual education programs produce better results than English immersion programs on key outcome variables. There is no significant evidence showing that bilingual programs impede the academic achievement of ELL students (National Research Council and Institute of Medicine, 1997; Suarez-Orozco & Suarez-Orozco, 2001). Furthermore, research indicates that it takes between two and eight years for ELL students to attain English fluency (Ma, 2002), and five years for ELLs to attain English language skills and academic achievement levels equal to their native English speaking peers (Thomas and Collier, 1997).

The findings from bilingual education support research on immigrant children and academic outcomes. Research in both areas has found evidence that maintenance of the home/family language is associated with higher levels of academic achievement. Research from bilingual education offers some evidence that the longer the native language is maintained as ELL students learn English, the better they will do in school.

Gender

The racial/ethnic academic achievement gap has been well documented: black and Latino students have lower levels of academic achievement compared to white and Asian students. It has also been well documented that girls/women outperform boys/men in school: girls- of all races/ethnicities- have higher grades through high school, with the exception that boys' grades tend to catch up to those of girls in high school where they tend to outperform them in math and science. Additionally, girls graduate from high school, matriculate into and graduate from college, and earn a graduate degree at higher rates than boys. These differences are particularly pronounced among girls and women of color who have significantly higher levels of academic achievement than boys and young men of color from elementary school through college and beyond. Clearly, men and boys of color are being left behind in a way that girls and women are not, in a way that is distinctly related to matters of race/ethnicity and gender. Notably, at any given moment in time there are more black and Latino boys and men in the juvenile detention or adult prison systems in the U.S. than are participating in education at any level, a gross disparity that also reflects greater spending on the U.S. prison system than education.

Gender is emerging as an important factor in shaping the pathways of immigrant youth, much as it is a key factor among the native-born. Across racial/ethnic groups, numerous studies of immigrant youth have found that girls from immigrant families have higher grades than boys (Brandon, 1991; Fuligni, 1997; Lee 2001; Lopez, 2002; Portes and Rumbaut, 2001; Waters 1996). The aforementioned studies by Fuligni (1997) and Lopez (2002) both found that girls had higher grades than boys, and that acculturation and generational status were negatively associated with academic motivation and grades, indicating a gender-by-acculturation interaction for grades. The previously described study by Portes and Rumbaut (2001) found numerous interrelated differences between boys and girls among diverse second generation Latino and Asian immigrant youth. They found that boys had lower grades, were less motivated towards and engaged in their schooling, had lesser career and educational aspirations, and were less likely to retain their parents' language. These findings are bolstered by various studies, among them the research of Rong and Brown (2001) who found that female immigrants from the Caribbean and Africa outperformed men academically; Waters' (1996) study of first and second generation black immigrant youth of immigrant families from Haiti and the West Indies who found that girls were more likely to graduate from high school than boys; and Brandon's (1991) study of Asian high school students which found that young women attained higher levels of academic achievement than boys.

In an effort to explain these disparities and gendered patterns, Suarez-Orozco & Baolian Qin (2002), reporting preliminary findings from the Harvard Longitudinal Immigrant Student Adaptation (LISA) study, found various differences, and some similarities, in the schooling experiences of immigrant Latino and Asian girls and boys from the Dominican Republic, Mexico, Central America, China, and Haiti. Results from their research found evidence of the well documented gender differences in academic performance, particularly as regards black and Latino boys in middle school and high school. On average boys had lower grades than girls, girls had significantly higher grades in language arts, and boys had lower grades in social studies, math and science. Importantly, among every national-origin group in the study boys had statistically lower grades than girls. Additionally, 24 percent of girls earned grades of B+ or higher compared to 16 percent of boys, whereas 11 percent of boys earned grades of D- or lower compared to 8 percent of girls.

To explain these results, the authors posit that boys' poorer academic performance may in part result from a combination of negative social relations in school: inadequate social support, negative and hostile experiences with teachers and school administrators (boys reported more racism at school, whereas girls were more likely to report positive relationships with adults at school), and low teacher expectations (teachers perceived girls much more positively than boys). The authors also propose that boys' relatively poorer academic performance may also result in part from low quality relationships outside of school, a lack of support, and the influence of peer pressure which may compromise immigrant boys' ability to do well in school. In sum, immigrant boys may be doing worse in school because they have lack adequate support, guidance and encouragement to achieve.

In an ethnographic study of urban Afro-Caribbean origin high school and college age young adults from the Dominican Republic, Haiti and the West Indies, Lopez (2003) endeavored to further explain the gender achievement gap. Although with an older age-group, by examining differences in schooling patterns the study helps to explain why racial/ethnic minority and immigrant boys/men have such disparate outcomes compared to girls/women. In her study, young men described low expectations, being placed in low curricular tracks, extensive problems with teachers, harsh discipline, rampant racism, and overall negative experiences and relationships within schools. Aware of these dynamics and low expectations, Lopez's concludes that the resentment of young men manifested in "willfull laziness," becoming academically disengaged and making no effort to earn high grades in school.

Boys' experiences in school were compounded by related experiences in the home, workplace, and in public. Socially and in public settings young men described being treated like criminals, thieves, and hoodlums by police and business owners. Additionally, young men described poor relationships and family ties, less social control and monitoring within the family compared to girls/women, a lack of adult responsibilities, such as childrearing and caring for family and the home, and more unsupervised time outside of the home, all unlike the girls/women in their families. Young men were in part ambivalent towards education because of the gender-based expectations placed on them by parents/family, culture, and peers, where getting an education was not associated with becoming a man or masculinity. Unlike the young men, young women were proud of their academic achievements and made efforts to attain their educational and career goals, reported strong and supportive family relationships and support networks, and an emphasis on the important of education. In sum, young women were hopeful and optimistic about their futures and how an education could help them achieve their dreams and goals, whereas young men were concerned about their futures and did not express the same kind of hope or optimism. Lopez proposes that "race-gender" experiences in schools, at home and at work, shape divergent "race-gender" outlooks. She describes these different race-gender experiences in schools as significant because they in turn shaped outlooks towards education and the future, namely the possibility and that, through education, they could achieve, succeed and move-up in the world.

Similar gender differences were found in research using CILS data (Feliciano & Rumbaut, 2005), and Rumbaut's study (2008) of CILS and IIMMLA data. Feliciano & Rumbaut (2005) examined the educational and occupational expectations and outcomes of young women and men of foreign-parentage over ten years. The study found that educational and occupational trajectories vary by class, ethnicity, and gender. Although both adolescent females and males had generally high expectations and goals, males began with slightly lower educational and occupational aspirations. Consistent with documented gender disparities in education, females were more likely to succeed in high school and complete an advanced degree, either because they held higher expectations for themselves or, similar to findings by Lopez (2003), because of their families' gendered expectation that girls should be "good." Second-generation young women were found to reject stereotypical gender roles and had high status aspirations, dreaming of having traditionally male-dominated professional occupations such as doctor or business executive.

However, among both young men and women expectations did not match up perfectly with outcomes. Although some study participants fell into the pathway "motivated achiever," the majority fell within the three pathways: "optimistic striver," "wishful thinker," and "defeatist drifter." Although the study was inconclusive as to whether aspirations will eventually be realized, because participants may still enter advanced degree programs, results suggest that the dreams of the second generation were most often deferred, dampened, or denied. The study raised important questions about how women of immigrant families are renegotiating their role, and how gender shapes immigrant children's transitions into adulthood.

In Rumbaut's study (2008) of educational mobility among 1.5 and second-generation young adults of diverse Latin American and Asian backgrounds, gender was found to play a significant role in determining educational mobility. Much like gender differences in education attainment among US-born men and women, in particular women and men of color, females reported higher educational achievement than their male counterparts, being more likely than males to have completed a college degree and not dropped out of high school. Incarceration, which was typically found among young men, and early childbearing were two factors that, not surprisingly, disrupted educational and occupational achievement, with females more likely to be negatively affected by having a child at an early age. Evident of the vicious cycle poor academic outcomes can lead to, and the importance of educational success, poor academic attainment in high school was found to be a predictor for incarceration and early pregnancy.

In sum, evidence indicates that immigrant racial/ethnic minority girls/women perform better academically than boys/men. This is consistent with studies which have found similar gendered trends among the general U.S. population. Evidence suggests that boys have poorer academic achievement and face unique challenges that girls do not, which put them at-risk for not doing well in school. Research indicates that poor academic performance is not an intrinsic male quality or that boys/men lack the drive, motivation, engagement, cognitive or behavioral qualities to achieve. Rather, evidence points to a variety of interrelated contextual factors that are specific to boys and which shape their educational pathways and thus future trajectories. Specifically, racial/ethnic minority boys contend with racism, prejudice, stereotypes and low expectations in and out of school, while not having sufficient guidance, support or encouragement to succeed academically. Future research should explore the distinct schooling experiences and outcomes of boys and girls, placing gender at the core of analysis as opposed to at the periphery, while taking these complex contextual influences into account.

Discussion

The research to date presents substantial evidence of a strong association between acculturation and academic outcomes. Importantly, the research has found a negative effect on academic outcomes with greater levels of acculturation, or with assimilation to U.S. culture. Studies indicate that with more acculturation (greater length of residency and/or greater use of English) grades tend to decrease; or the more assimilated children are, the poorer their academic outcomes.

These studies have observed more optimal outcomes in less-acculturated children than in white majority children or more acculturated children of the same immigrant, national, or pan/ethnic group. Acculturation, particularly assimilation- notably greater use of English coupled with loss of the home/family language- seems to lead to poorer academic outcomes among children of immigrant families. Conversely, maintenance of the home/family culture and language seems to function as a protective factor for immigrant children, which is associated with better outcomes. In short, contrary to dominant beliefs, the more Americanized children of immigrant families are, the poorer their academic outcomes. These findings are important because they are in conflict with traditional, prevailing theories of immigrant incorporation and assimilation; theories which state that immigrants who are more acculturated, those who speak English and adopt "American" cultural ways, will have better educational, health, behavioral and socioeconomic outcomes.

These highly provocative and controversial findings have been termed the "immigrant paradox." The immigrant paradox refers to the counterintuitive finding that more recent and less acculturated immigrants have more optimal educational, health, and behavioral outcomes than more acculturated immigrants, or than would be expected given their low socioeconomic status and other risk factors present. This is difficult to understand because as people acculturate to life in the US they tend to use more English, develop social networks, acquire social capital, and earn more money, factors that are associated with higher levels of academic achievement. Thus, the immigrant paradox is the phenomenon that foreign birth and less acculturation appears to be a protective factor, and that increased length of residency/subsequent generations and greater acculturation and use of English is associated with a variety of negative educational, health, and behavioral indicators.

Interestingly, studies to date have also found that among immigrant youth and young adults, girls/women outperform boys/men academically. Some studies have also identified provocative associations between and differences by gender and acculturation, indicating a gender-by-acculturation interaction (Fuligni, 1997; Lopez, 2002). This emerging literature suggest another layer and set of contextual influences that may shape academic outcomes in addition to immigration or racial/ethnic or language minority status. These findings also point to the possibility that gender may function as a moderating variable that changes the relationship between acculturation and language and academic performance, or schooling experiences and academic performance.

Furthermore, there are profound differences in outcomes and experiences within groups (eg: based on country of origin, race/ethnicity, age, gender, length of residency in the US), which have been found in the research literature. Thus, no one model can fit all immigrant groups. However, most research that has studied racial/ethnic minority groups has used a comparative approach and few studies have employed within-group designs. The difference being that within-group studies would allow for the examination of individual groups on their own terms, instead of compared to their similarities and differences from other groups (Phinney & Landin, 1998). Thus, there is limited understanding about how the particular realities and characteristics of distinct groups shape development and academic performance.

Overall, the evidence suggests that immigrants lose something over time in this country, and that this is associated with various measures of health and well being that, in most cases, deteriorate over time. These processes and outcomes are the result of various nested contextual factors, but may in part be the result of gendered pathways, resources and experiences that present different assets and vulnerabilities for girls/women and boys/men. These contextual influences can pose unique challenges that shape developmental and academic trajectories based on gender. Research is needed to understand the resources and vulnerabilities particular to boys/girls, how and why these paradoxical and disparate outcomes occur, as well as how early in the life span they can be observed.

CHAPTER 4
Guiding Theories

Middle childhood is a historically understudied period in human development. In particular, little is known about children of immigrant families during this stage. This research adds to the literature in this area as it is a study of the impact of language on academic performance among a sample of children of immigrant families from the Dominican Republic in middle childhood.

Life is not experienced in a bubble. Multiple interrelated contexts impact growth, development, and thus academic performance, and the characteristics of these different contexts often must be negotiated and balanced. Thus, this study does not take a single-context approach. Rather, it situates children within their cultural and familial contexts to more comprehensively understand academic performance. The theoretical perspectives that framed this research were ecological theory (Bronfenbrenner, 1979) and multiple worlds theory (Phelan, Davidson, & Yu, 1991, 1998), as well as Berry's theory of acculturation (Berry, et al., 1992), and the work of Portes and Rumbaut (2001).

Ecological and Multiple Worlds Theories

Considered the father of ecological theory, Bronfenbrenner (1979) argued that human development was the result of evolving interactions between individuals and their environments. He proposed that development was the result of a complex of nested and interconnected settings and systems that shape development. Ecological theory is thus a theory of environmental interconnections and their collective impact on development. The theory emphasizes that development is not the processes themselves- such as "thinking" or "learning"- but the context, how those processes are perceived, understood and how they change as a function of a person's exposure and interactions within their environment. Thus, scientific understanding of the processes and outcomes of human development requires investigation of their many interconnected environments.

Earlier analyses framed child development and observed outcomes as the interaction between "nature" and "nurture". New research in neurobiology, which lends credence to ecological theory, has found that brain development is not the result of nature or nurture, but rather an ongoing and constantly evolving interaction among an individual's genetic factors within their environments - or development in context (National Research Council and Institute of Medicine, 2000). Ecological theory proposes just that, and stresses that people can not be understood outside of their particular contexts. Development is seen as the result of an individual's interactions with their environment. These contextual interactions shape processes and give rise to individual outcomes.

Multiple worlds theory (Phelan, Davidson, & Yu, 1991, 1998), builds on ecological theory. The work is based on studies of adolescents and presents the concept of "worlds," such as the school, family, and peer group, contexts which have specific activities and require management and organization, and which together must be balanced by the individual. Phelan et al (1991) define the term "world" as "cultural knowledge and behavior found within the boundaries of students' families, peer groups, and schools; we presume that each world contains values and beliefs, expectations, actions, and emotional responses familiar to insiders" (p.225). The theory presents a model for understanding the interrelationships between the different contexts of development, and particularly how meaning and understanding from each of these worlds come together and impact learning and engagement in school. Central to multiple worlds theory is the understanding that, because different contexts have culturally specific knowledge and meaning systems, such as language and customs, moving among different contexts often necessitates knowledge and skills as different worlds are defined by different cultural standards and values. Phelan et al (1991) describe how minority adolescents often must deal with two culturally distinct worlds- that of the home/family, and that of the school. Multiple worlds theory proposes that youth must learn to negotiate their different contexts and, to be successful in school, they must learn how to balance their different worlds. Phelan et al. found that students employ different adaptive strategies to move among worlds and interact in different contexts and settings, and that students' success in school is largely contingent upon how well they learn to negotiate their different worlds, or contexts.

Importance of Language

Ecological theory and multiple worlds theory offer appropriate frameworks for thinking about the proposed research. Children of immigrant families from the Dominican Republic face certain challenges that are specific to their location as an immigrant minority group in the social stratification system of the United States, outside of the dominant US mainstream culture. Children of immigrants and their families struggle with a host of issues as they acculturate and to life in the U.S. and make adaptations necessary for life and survival in different contexts. The children in this study are part of a transnational Dominican community living in Providence, Rhode Island and throughout the US, which is characterized by frequent and regular travel, communication and other exchanges between the United States and the Dominican Republic. Consequently, these children are bi-national because, although they live in the US, they live in and between two countries, and consequently two cultures. The children in this study live in a community that can be characterized as a Spanish-speaking Latino ethnic enclave within the city of Providence. They face the challenge of living in, navigating, and balancing, two very different worlds- that of their families/homes and community that is culturally distinct from the mainstream culture of the schools they attend. In addition, they struggle with having to live in and use two culturally distinct and contextually specific languages- Spanish and English. Language is integral to the process of acculturation for immigrants. Their linguistic adaptations- how much English and/or Spanish they speak- are informed by the two very different cultures they straddle. Children of immigrant families from the Dominican Republic are part of a Latino community where their Dominican culture and the Spanish language is maintained and used in day-to-day life. However, these children attend mainstream US schools that require linguistic adaptations. How they manage these linguistic differences should thus impact their performance in school.

Acculturation

The study used Berry's theory of acculturation to understand the linguistic adaptations of the children in this study. Acculturation is a complex construct, the level and type of which has been measured multiple ways. Length of residency, place of birth, and English language skills have served as the principle proxies for acculturation in the research literature, and have been used to measure degree and type of acculturation. Berry identifies four acculturation types: biculturalism, assimilation, marginalization, and separation (Berry, et al., 1992). In brief, biculturalism is when a person possesses the language, skills and knowledge, has values, and exhibits behaviors that are specific to the dominant culture as well as those belonging to the home culture. In effect, such a person is fluent in the dominant, in this case American, culture, as well as fluent in the home/family culture, in this case of the Dominican Republic. Using language as a proxy, biculturalism can be equated with bilingualism. Assimilation is when a person is solely versed in the dominant (American,) culture. Such a person has not learned, or perhaps has not been exposed to, has been prevented from acquiring, or has given-up learning, the particulars of the home/family culture. Assimilation is equal to being English-monolingual. Separation is the opposite of assimilation, and is when a person is solely versed in the home/family culture, and lacks knowledge of or proficiency with the dominant (American) culture. Separation is equivalent to being Spanish-monolingual. Marginalization is when a person lacks a foothold in either the dominant or home/family culture. Such a person will lack the language, as well as skills, knowledge, values, and behaviors of both the dominant and home culture. Such persons would lack both English and Spanish language skills and would be effectively neither "here" nor "there". It is similar to what Portes and Rumbaut (2001) and Suarez-Orozco and Suarez-Orozco (2001) call dissonant acculturation, as evidenced by the prevalence of deviant behaviors and involvement in self-destructive youth sub-culture among marginalized adolescents.

Immigrants and children of immigrants adjust to life in the US using different strategies and following different paths. Some assimilate and become American, some become bicultural, some remain entrenched in the native culture, and some acculturate to the fringes of society, to a youth sub-culture, effectively excluded from both mainstream US society and the home/family culture. The four different acculturation types identified by Berry are consistent with the empirical evidence to date, in particular the findings of Portes and Rumbaut (2001) and Suarez-Orozco and Suarez-Orozco (2001). Importantly, Portes and Rumbaut's (2001) suggestion of selective acculturation as the preferred strategy for immigrant children, is in keeping with Berry's concept of biculturalism. The proposed research seeks to add to the extant literature by studying acculturation and its impact on academic outcomes among elementary school aged children in middle childhood.

Language has been used in the literature as an index of acculturation. In and of itself, language is a proxy for how acculturated someone is. Acculturation is not just length or residency or the amount of time spent in the US, it is exposure, learning, the social aspects of acculturation as well; thus language is a measure for one's ability to read English which directly impact one's ability to engage in such basic and necessary tasks as take a road test, complete a job application, and buy groceries, among other things, which in turn are all important for education. Because it is so important, language has often been used as a marker of acculturation.

The concept of acculturation is central to this research. However, acculturation is a multidimensional construct that captures many factors, among them cultural practices (such as the religion and the kind of food one eats, among others), behaviors, attitudes, and feelings, as well as language. John Berry, considered the father of psychological acculturation, defined acculturation as a process that unfolds from contact between groups, and characterizes how a person responds to and orients him or herself to a changing cultural context. Acculturation is a process that results in certain socio-cultural adaptations, or the long term ways in which a person rearranges her/his life, and how well s/he can settle-down and manage day to day life in their new cultural context (Berry, et al., 1992). As such, acculturation is the process by which immigrants and their children adapt to life in a new country that is culturally dissimilar from where they or their families came. One key aspect of this is the linguistic adaptations people make through the acculturation process, which was the specific focus of this research.

This study was focused on linguistic acculturation, and not overall psychological acculturation, which includes behaviors feelings, and many other aspects and sociocultural dimensions which are beyond the scope of this study. This study was not focused on the totality of dimensions which characterize the acculturation process or outcomes, but rather linguistic acculturation only.

Traditionally, immigration, biculturalism, and bilingualism have been conceptualized as liabilities that are certain to have a negative impact on development and educational outcomes. As such, in this period of high immigration and growth in the Latino population, not being in mainstream classes but rather being a bilingual education or English as a second language (ESL) student, especially one who speaks Spanish, are frequently regarded as liabilities. The use of a language other than English in school in and of itself is often believed to put children at risk for academic failure. For example, if bilingual education students do not do well, it is because they were in bilingual education and speak Spanish, implying that the educational program type has a direct effect on academic outcomes. At the same time, coming from a family where a "foreign language," particularly Spanish, is spoken, is often perceived as not just a threat to national identity, but also as something that in and of itself poses certain risks for children in the home. A 1995 Texas divorce case illustrates this point. In that case in Amarillo, Texas, a judge, presiding over a child-custody hearing as part of a divorce case, ordered the mother, a US citizen of Mexican descent, to speak English to her daughter. When she told him that she only spoke English to her, he said: "[You are] abusing that child and relegating her to the position of a house maid." and "It's not in her best interest to be ignorant." The judge threatened to terminate the mother's custody unless she spoke to her daughter in English (Gonzalez, 2006, p.206). This is an example of the widespread belief in this country that the language of the home (especially if it is Spanish and the family is Latino) has a direct and negative effect on outcomes.

The latest research suggests that bilingualism is not a liability, but rather might be an asset for immigrant children. The possible benefits of being bilingual are at the core of this research, which frames bilingualism not as a risk, but rather as an asset (Portes & Rumbaut, 2001). It was hypothesized that bilingualism (use of both English and Spanish) would be associated with greater success in school.

Biculturalism is understood as a logical and appropriate adaptation because it allows immigrant children to maintain their home language and culture while learning the English they need for school. It was anticipated that assimilation would not help these children succeed in school, thus it was hypothesized that academic performance may decrease with greater use of English coupled with loss of the home language. Assimilation was not foreseen as the best option because these children live in two cultures and have to bridge two very different worlds. They need bilingual skills to effectively function in both. It was expected that some use of the home language, as well as knowledge of the dominant (school) language, would be necessary for these children to do well, and thus it was predicted that bilingualism would emerge as optimal for this group of children.

CHAPTER 5
The Nuts and Bolts of this Study

The research was a combined cross sectional and longitudinal study of children of immigrant families from the Dominican Republic living in Providence, RI. The study was a quantitative secondary data analysis of data from the study *Children of Immigrants Development in Context* (CIDC).

Research Design and Methodology

Research Question and Hypotheses
This research sought to understand the impact of language acculturation, specifically child language preference, on academic performance. It also examined the language spoken in the home and the language spoken in the school to determine if there was an association between those two contexts and either child language preference or academic performance. The language spoken by the mother was deemed to be the best gauge of the home language, thus mother's language was used as an indicator for this measure. The primary research question was:

Can language acculturation explain some of the variation in academic performance for children of immigrant families from the Dominican Republic?

Four hypotheses were tested to explore this primary research question:

H1. Children who are bilingual will have better levels of academic performance compared to children who are assimilated.

H_a: Children who are assimilated will have poorer levels of academic performance compared to children who are bilingual.

H2. The language spoken by the mother/in the home will have a direct effect on academic performance.

H_a: The language spoken by the mother/in the home will have an indirect effect on academic performance, working through the child as a mediator.

H3: The language spoken in school will have a direct effect on academic performance.

H_a: The language spoken in the school will have an indirect effect on academic performance, working through the child as a mediator.

H4: Sex will moderate the way language preference relates to academic performance

H_a: Sex will not moderate the way language preference relates to academic performance.

Sample

The research was limited to the 139 Dominican children. The sample consisted of 65 boys and 74 girls in two age cohorts.

Measures

Grades

The CIDC study data contained numerical grades on a scale of 0-12 (representative of letter grades from F to A+). Each letter grade was equivalent to one number grade:

12 =A+	8 = B	5 = C	2 = D
11 =A	7 = B-	4 = C-	1 = D-
10 =A-	6 = C+	3 = D+	0 = F
9 = B+			

Numbers were rounded to determine equivalent letter grades for numerical grades. Grades were available for reading, writing, math, science and social studies subject areas.

Academic Performance

In the cross sectional and longitudinal analyses, academic performance was measured by using three year GPA as well as GPA for each year of the study. In the structural equation modeling, academic performance was measured by using GPA in each of the three years of the study as well as the teacher ratings from year three.

Academic achievement was used interchangeably with academic performance.

Primary Language Preference

Child language preference was a central measure for this research. Child language preference was based on five questions from the child interview in year 2 for which the response was either Spanish, both the same, or English. The measures were:

1. Which language do you like to speak more, English or Spanish, or do you like them both the same?
2. Do you like to have people speak to you in English or Spanish, or do you like them both the same?
3. Do you like to watch TV and movies in English or Spanish, or do you like them both the same?
4. Would you like to have your teachers teach in English or Spanish, or do you like them both the same?
5. When people read or tell you stories, what do you like more: to hear stories in English or in Spanish, or do you like them both the same?

Of the five questions, the question on TV was thought to be inherently biased as most popular children's television programs/cartoons are in English, and therefore this question was deemed not an accurate reflection of language preference because children probably prefer a particular television program regardless of the language it is in. For these reasons, the question on TV was not used in the analyses.

In order to develop a scale with which to examine a theory of language acculturation, each of the four Primary Language Preference measures was treated as ordinal variables, If language acculturation is thought of as a linear process and bilingualism as a transitional period leading up to full (cultural and linguistic) assimilation into English monolingualism (Hakuta, 1986, p. 7), this would mean that as children start to assimilate they start as Spanish monolingual speakers, then become bilingual, and finally become English monolingual prefering English only- the desired end goal of assimilation. This theory equates Spanish language preference with being not assimilated, bilingualism as being in the transitionary period that leads to assimilation, and English preference as being assimilated. To capture this trend the language preference variables were coded on a scale of 1-3, where 1=Spanish monolingual (not assimilated), 2=bilingual, and 3=English monolingual (assimilated). Conceptualizing these variables in this manner, allowed more sophisticated analyses, making it possible to understand how greater assimilation could impact academic performance. This would not have been possible if these variables had been treated as categorical.

Binary Language Preference

Binary Language Preference measures of Bilingual and English preference were created from all four of the Primary Language Preference variables. In this case, each Primary Language Preference Measure was recoded into two dummy variables, where children who reported English preference were coded as preferring English only (1=yes, 0=no), and those who reported Spanish or bilingual preference were coded as having bilingual preference (1=yes, 0=no). Very few children reported Spanish language preference in any of the language preference categories and it was not possible to examine the relationship between Spanish language preference and academic performance. Thus, the children who reported Spanish preference were collapsed with those who reported preferring both languages equally for each of the four Primary Language Preference questions. Each of these children reported speaking a language other than English, namely Spanish, which clearly indicates they have at least some grasp of both languages. Thus, for these two binary measures, this small number of children was coded as having a bilingual preference/not preferring English only.

Composite Score of Language Preference

A composite measure of language preference was created by collapsing two of the Primary Language Preference questions (1) language the child prefers to speak, and (2) language in which the child prefers to be spoken to, and scoring them. These two indicators were deemed to be the simplest and thus the best indicators of language preference when considered together. Three separate variables were created for Spanish, bilingual, and English preference depending on the response. These three variables were:

- Prefers to speak and be spoken to in English
- Prefers to speak and be spoken to in Spanish
- Prefers to speak and be spoken to bilingually/in both languages equally

Each of the measures was coded on a scale of 0-2 to measure none, moderate and high language preference for each language preference measure. If a child reported the same language/s for both Primary Language Preference questions, for example English, then s/he received a 2 for the English Composite Score of Language Preference and 0 for each of the Bilingual and Spanish Composite Score of Language Preference measures. This would mean that a child had high English preference and no Spanish or bilingual preference. If, for example, a child reported preferring to speak in both languages equally/bilingually but to be spoken to in Spanish, s/he received a 1 for the Bilingual Composite Score of Language Preference measure, a 1 for the Spanish Composite Score Language Preference measure, and a 0 for the English Composite Score of Language Preference measure. This would mean that a child had a moderate English and Spanish preference, but no bilingual preference. A hypothetical example of how this variable was scored is provided in Table 2.

With this measure it was possible to assess the level of language preference for each Composite Score of Language Preference measure, as 0=no preference, 1=moderate preference, and 2=high language preference. As a scored measure, these variables were treated as ordinal variables to measure the degree of language preference in each category as well as to capture scaled increases in language preference.

This allowed for the examination of greater preference for a particular language on academic performance.

Bilingual Preference

For each of the language preference measures (Primary, Binary, and Composite), a bilingual child was defined as a child who preferred both Spanish and English equally.

Table 2: Example of Scoring for Composite Score of Language Preference Measure

	Primary Language Preference measure		Composite Score of Language Preference: Prefers to speak and be spoken to in:		
Child	Prefers to speak	Prefers to be spoken to	Spanish	Bilingual	English
Child A	English	English	0	0	2
Child B	Bilingual	Spanish	1	1	0
Child C	Bilingual	Bilingual	0	2	0
Child D	Bilingual	English	0	1	1

Assimilated/English Preference

For each of the language preference measures (Primary, Binary, and Composite), an assimilated child was defined as child who preferred English.

Linguistic Fit

Language preference was used to gauge linguistic fit between the home and the school. This measure was created to explore linguistic congruence between the child's home and the school. This was measured by first calculating the difference between (1) the language in which the child prefers to be spoken to, which was interpreted as a strong proxy for the language in which the child prefers to be spoken to at home, and (2) the language the child prefers the teacher teach in. Linguistic fit was a binary variable based on whether there was a difference between the responses to the two questions. To calculate it the response to the second question (what language the child prefers the teacher teach in) was subtracted from the first (the language in which the child prefers to be spoken to). Therefore, a difference of 0=no difference, and for anything other than zero the binary measure was coded as 1=some difference between the two contexts.

As there was no survey question that asked the children what language they prefer to use with their parents, the question on what language the child prefers to be spoken to in was deemed a good proxy for home linguistic preference as the language they prefer to be spoken to in is likely the language they prefer their parents speak to them in. This is especially probable given that these are young children, age ten or younger, for whom their parents and families comprise the majority of their close relationships and personal interactions. Therefore, it is likely that their parents are who came to mind when the children were asked the question, as their parents/family are probably the people they mostly speak to outside of school.

Mother's language use and comfort/language spoken in the home
Measures of the mother's language use and comfort were used to examine the impact of the mother's language/the language of the home. These measures are from questions from the parent interview in year 2. Mother's language comfort encompassed four questions for which the scaled response was either 0=don't speak English, 1=uncomfortable, 2=comfortable, 3=very comfortable. The four questions were:

1. Do you speak to your neighbors in English?
2. Do you talk to people at work in English?
3. Do you talk on the phone in English?
4. Do you speak English with the people at your child's school?

Mother's language use was based on two questions for which the scaled response was 1=only Spanish, 2=more Spanish than English, 3=both Spanish and English the same, 4=more English than Spanish, 5=only English. The two questions were:

1. What language/s do you speak?
2. What language/s do you speak to the child?

Socio-economic Status

A measure of socio-economic status (SES) was calculated by summing the responses to a series of questions from the parent interview in year 2. Four of the five indicators was first transformed into a standard score (z-score) and then the four were summed together along with the fifth indicator, single parent. As single parent status was a dichotomous variable, a 1 was added if the parent was a single parent. The five indicators used to measure socioeconomic status were annual income, mother's years of schooling, parent involvement in their child's education, the number of places the family has lived in since the child started school, and whether the child lived in a single parent household (see Appendix A for exact measures and coding).

Some non-traditional measures were used to calculate SES as they were deemed to be particularly relevant to this study. This was done in order to "think outside the box" and capture some of the nuances of socioeconomic status that could be lost by only using traditional measures that do not account for other closely related factors. SES and social location are intimately related and what these two factors mean for children, what their effects might be on their performance in school, is what this measure of SES tried to capture. It is hypothesized that involvement in education is associated with SES as well as social location, and thus academic performance: the more well-off families are the more likely they are to be involved in their child's education. Much as income increases with years of schooling, so it is likely that parent involvement in education will increase with greater education and higher incomes. Growing up in a single parent household has been shown to be predictive of academic performance. Mobility was included as it is hypothesized that increased mobility is associated with SES: less well off families, such as those whom contend with unstable housing, are more likely to move more, whereas more socioeconomically stable families are less likely to move, or remain in the same home for longer periods of time during their child's education. By including these appropriate albeit non-traditional measures, it was possible to calculate a comprehensive measure of SES appropriate for this research.

The language spoken in school
Child's class type over the three years was used as an indicator of the language the child speaks in school. Children were in the following two types of classes:

- Bilingual: both Spanish and English used in the classroom
- English mainstream: English only used in the classroom

These data were available for each of the three years individually. To capture the language spoken in school for three years, the above two categories were used to measure the language spoken in school when children were in each type of class for all of the three years. In addition, the following category was created to measure the language spoken in school for children who switched classes during the three years:

- Transitioned: children transitioned from a bilingual education class to an English only mainstream class over the three years.

No children transitioned from an English mainstream class to a bilingual class.

Analytic Methods

Tests of mean group differences were first conducted to determine if children in the linguistic groups were different in significant ways. Results found no significant mean differences between bilingual and assimilated children, indicating equivalency between groups. The variables examined were parent income, poverty level, mother's age, single or two-parent family, mother's level of education (years), attitudes on parent involvement in education, whether parents own or rent their home, parents number of previous US addresses, number of places lived in since child started school, child place of birth, and the number of minutes the child spends on homework.

A descriptive stage followed by four analytical steps, bivariate analyses, multivariate regression analysis, a longitudinal analysis, and structural equation modeling, were used to answer the research question. These four levels of analysis were conducted to examine things three different ways: bivariate analyses were used to explore non-directional associations among variables; multivariate regression analysis was the simplest of the three models that provided a glimpse into one moment in time; the longitudinal analysis examined things over time; and the structural equation modeling allowed for more complex modeling with the use of latent variables. These three analyses were similar, but the models complement each other as they offer three different perspectives.

Bivariate analyses consisted of correlations and tests of mean group differences. Pearson's Correlation Coefficient (Pearson's r) and Spearman's rho were both used as correlation measures. Ordinary least squares (OLS) multivariate regression with a 95 percent confidence interval was used to estimate the model that best predicted academic performance among children. To build the regression model, independent variables were entered stepwise manually. Cases were excluded listwise to handle missing values. The longitudinal analysis explored time trends and modeled long term effects when controlling for time. Using linear mixed model analysis, fixed effects of panel data were tested using Type III sums of squares. Estimates were calculated using restricted maximum likelihood to handle missing values.

Structural Equation Modeling
Structural equation modeling (SEM) was the central analytical method of this research. SEM was used to build-regression like models using latent variables. Similar to confirmatory factor analysis and path analysis, SEM is a theory-driven method used to estimate models with linear relationships among variables (MacCallum & Austin, 2000). Thus, the model tested was developed based on theory which drives the measurement of the constructs and the associations among them.

The variables in a structural equation model can be both directly observed and latent. Latent variables, such as "acculturation," cannot be directly observed and measured, and are instead theoretical constructs that can be represented by indicator variables serving as proxies. As a structural equation model is a theoretical model as opposed to an experimental model, the relationships among the set of latent and measurable variables in the model are hypothetical. A structural equation model is commonly used to test substantive hypotheses that consist of relationships that are by nature linear. The model is comprised of a series of linear relationships among variables, and can be either directional or non-directional. Directional relationships denote the influence of one variable on another variable in a specific direction, whereas non-directional relationships are merely correlational and do not indicate any directional influence between variables. The current study built a directional model.

Structural equation models assess associations among variables in order to understand a complex construct, as opposed to measuring the effects of independent variables on dependent variables. In SEM directionality is not tantamount to causality; rather the direction of effect corresponds to a theory. In SEM, "effects" imply causality, but it is important to understand that this type of "causality" does not infer a "causal relationship" in the traditional sense, but rather denotes the direction of effect. Thus, SEM does not test for correlations between "independent" and "dependent" variables in the traditional sense. Structural equation models have no independent and dependent variables, but rather exogenous and endogenous variables, which are conceptually similar to independent and dependent variables, respectively. An exogenous variable is a variable that is not "caused" by another variable in the model and usually "causes" one or more variables in the model. An endogenous variable is a variable that is caused by one or more variables in the model, and may also cause another endogenous variable in the structural equation model. The structural equation modeling was an effort to determine if the latent construct "child language preference," could be created as an estimate of associations among variables, as opposed to testing for the effect of certain independent variable on a dependent variable as measured by the correlations between them.

Methodologically, SEM is equally about the research process and the outcomes. This means that the emphasis is not solely on the outcome itself. The process of developing the model, and the model that is created, are just as important as the findings.

Methodological Limitations of SEM
This study was not designed to determine causality. SEM is by definition a method that seeks to understand associations, the unique relationships among observed variables and latent constructs. This research sought to understand the relationships between language and academic performance as it pertains to the children in this sample.

Thus the research findings are not generalizeable to the larger Dominican, immigrant, or Latino populations. Rather, they are generalizeable to larger process and theoretical principles. This is consistent with and supported by the chosen method, as SEM is a theory driven method designed to explore substantive hypotheses to better understand the processes and mechanisms involved as well as the outcomes.

Most statistical methods for SEM assume that the data are continuous variables. However, not all the variables used in the structural equation modeling were continuous. This means that the model built explains less than would a model built strictly of continuous variables.

Modeling Process and Data Analysis Plan
The structural equation modeling was a multi-stage analytical process that began with a theory and consisted of (1) developing the measurement models and (2) fitting the structural model. The theoretical basis for this research is that language has an impact on academic performance, and more specifically that child language has a direct effect on academic performance. SEM was also used to explore whether the language spoken by the mother/in the home and the language spoken in the school have either a direct or indirect effect on academic performance. This was done to explore competing theories of whether home or school language has an effect on child language or academic performance.

Step 1: Building the measurement models
The first step in this process required building the measurement models for each of the contexts of interest, namely the three exogenous latent variables child language preference, the language spoken by the mother/in the home, and the language spoken in the school. Throughout the process of building the individual measurement models and later fitting the structural model, maximum likelihood was used to estimate means and intercepts for missing data. For each of the three exogenous latent variables in the model, a measurement model with observed indicator variables was created. The measurement models were developed independently of each other. This is done in order to achieve

the best linear combination of variables that come together to measure the construct.

Stage 2: Fitting the Structural Model

A structural equation model was fit using the latent variables specified when the measurement models were built. The structural equation modeling sought to examine a theory of associations as illustrated in the theoretical model in Figure 4.1 below. In the figure, the large circles are the latent constructs (each representing a measurement model comprised of observed variables) and the rectangles are observed variables, which here represent controls.

Figure 1: Theoretical model

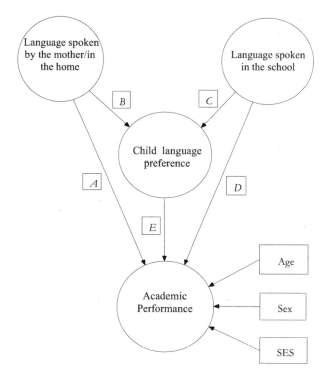

As indicated by the arrows in Figure 1, this study sought to build a directional model testing multiple paths, with the arrows in the theoretical model denoting the direction of effects to be tested, as denoted by the italic capital letters A through E in Figure 1:

A: Language spoken by the mother/in the home has a direct effect on academic performance

B: Language spoken by the mother/in the home has an indirect effect on academic performance working through the child as a mediator.

C: Language used in the school has an indirect effect on academic performance working through the child as a mediator.

D: Language spoken in the school has a direct effect on academic performance.

E: The child's language has a direct effect on academic performance.

It is important to emphasize that this is the theoretical model that this research sought to examine. This study is theory driven, and SEM is employed to test a theory. It is therefore the final structural model may not match the hypothesized theoretical model.

Parameter Estimates and Model Fit

To build both the measurement and structural models, the data are fit to the model to yield parameter estimates and fit statistics. To estimate a model, the data are fit to the model by converting the data into correlations and covariances. The final model consists of parameter estimates of the strength of associations among variables and statistics of overall model fit. These indicate whether the theory fits the observed data. The parameter estimates determine if a particular path is significant or not, and the measures of overall model fit determine the strength of the overall model. There is no single definitive fit statistic in SEM, thus four fit statistics were used as criteria to assess model fit: (1) Chi-square, (2) The Comparative Fit Index (CFI), (3) Normed Fit Index NFI, and (4) Root Mean Square Error of Approximation (RMSEA). The Chi-square distribution tests the hypothesis that the model does not fit the data. Thus, in SEM it is desirable to reject the hypothesis and have a value of >.05 (rather than ≤.05). In addition, Chi Square is a measure that reflects combinations of variables and cases in the data, and is therefore sensitive to both sample size and the number of variables in the model. Thus, the interplay of these two factors can throw off the model as reflected in a small Chi Square. The CFI and NFI are measure of how well the model fits on a scale of 1-100, and in the literature a measure of good fit ranges between .9 and 1. However, the NFI may underestimate fit for a small sample size and therefore the more liberal cutoff of .8 is sometimes used to determine model fit. RMSEA is a measure of how much error there is in the model and should be small, specifically <.06, which would indicate less than 5 percent error. However, an error of ≤.08 is acceptable (Gefen et al., 2000). Generally, if one of these fit statistics indicates that the model holds, all four will indicate that the model holds. However, that is not always the case, and it is accepted to accept a model if three of the four fit statistics indicate the model fits.

Summary

Although structural equation modeling was the central analytic component of this research, the three levels of analysis conducted provide complementary models that worked together to understand whether language acculturation could explain some of the variability in academic performance among this sample of children. Specifically, it was designed to understand whether less bilingual children outperformed assimilated children, *or* whether assimilated children outperformed bilingual children. In addition, the research explored whether the mother's language use and comfort/the language spoken in the home, and the language spoken in the school have a direct or indirect effect on academic performance. The results presented in the next chapter will describe in detail the associations between child language preference and academic performance uncovered through this study.

CHAPTER 6

Modeling Language, Gender, and Academic Performance

Analyses sought to answer the question, Can some of the variation in academic performance for children of immigrant families from the Dominican Republic be explained by differences in language acculturation? To this end, regression models, linear mixed models, and structural equation models were created. This chapter will begin with a brief description of the children in the study. Subsequently, each of the four analytical steps, their respective analyses, procedures, and results will be detailed, followed by a summary of the key findings and limitations.

Descriptive Statistics

Sample characteristics
The 139 children in the sample were fairly evenly divided between boys and girls in both age groups, as illustrated in Table 3 below:

Table 3: Sample Distribution by Sex and Cohort

Children	Younger Cohort	Older Cohort	Total
Girls	40	34	74
Boys	31	34	65
Total	71	68	139

Language, Gender, and Academic Performance

The majority of the children were second generation (born in the US to at least one foreign born parent). There was a fairly even split between US and foreign born boys and girls. As illustrated in Table 4, there was also a fairly equal distribution of US-born and foreign born children by cohort.

Table 4: Child's Place of Birth and Parents' Place of Birth, by Sex and Cohort (percentages)

Children	Child 's country of birth		Mother's country of birth		Father's country of birth	
	US	Foreign	US	Foreign	US	Foreign
Sex						
Girls	67.1%	32.9%	5.7%	94.3%	0%	0%
Boys	71.9%	28.1%	4.4%	95.6%	6.7%	93.3%
Cohort						
Younger Cohort	72.5%	27.5%	4.3%	95.7%	0%	0%
Older Cohort	66.2%	33.8%	5.8%	94.2%	5.8%	94.2%

Table 5: Mother's Language(s) and Language(s) Spoken in the Home (percentages)

Language(s)	Language(s) spoken by mother	Language(s) mother uses to speak to child
Only Spanish	21.0%	49.0%
More Spanish than English	53.0%	15.3%
Both Spanish and English equally	23.0%	18.4%
More English than Spanish	3.0%	7.1%
Only English	0%	10.2%

For children for whom data on parents' place of birth were available, the majority of children had two parents who were born abroad (most in the Dominican Republic, with a few born in another Latin American country). Reflective of the parents' immigrant status, most of the mothers spoke Spanish or more Spanish than English, and in particular spoke mostly Spanish with the child. As presented in Table 5, this indicates the majority of the children were growing up in either Spanish dominant or bilingual households.

The vast majority of the children had a bilingual preference. As indicated in Table 6 below, this was especially true of the language the child prefers to speak and the language in which the child prefers to be spoken to. However, the majority of children preferred the teacher teach in English.

Data on the parents' place of birth and mothers' language as well as the following descriptive results were available for 72 percent of children. These data help to contextualize the background of the children, and illustrate their demographic characteristics and families' social location.

Table 6: Childs Primary Language Preference Distribution (percentages)

Language Preference	Spanish	English	Spanish and English equally; Bilingual
Language prefers to speak	2%	32%	74%
Language prefers to be spoken to	6%	28%	74%
Language prefers teacher teach	10%	58%	40%
Language prefers to hear stories	4%	52%	52%

Approximately half of the children, 21 girls and 27 boys, were being raised by a single mother. This is consistent with research by Kasinitz, et al. (2008) which found that Caribbean immigrants had a higher rate of single-parent households compared to other immigrant groups. With this exception, the children possessed many of the characteristics common to immigrant families, namely they were poor/ low income and their mother's had low levels of education. Among children for whom parents reported income information (86%), three quarters were in families that had annual incomes below $20,000 (the poverty level in 2000 was $17,500 for a family of 4), and only 4 children were in families where the annual income was $40,000 or more (200% poverty in 2000 for a family of 4). This is probably due to large percentage of single mother families with possibly only one wage earner. Additionally, the rate of home ownership was low, as only 16% of parents reported owning their own home. Mobility was also high as on average families had lived at four different addresses since coming to the Providence area, ranging from none prior to the current address to a high of twenty. Only 33 percent of families had lived in the same address since the child started school. On average, mothers had 11 years of schooling, with a range of 2 to 22 years, and of whom only 27 percent had completed 12 years of school, which is equal in the number of years to completing high school in the US.

Grades
The vast majority of children (n=114, 82%) had complete grades data for all three years of the study. Data were imputed for children missing one year of grades data (n=12, 8.6%). Data were not imputed for children missing more than one year of grades. Grade imputation used a within-subject mean replacement based on grades for the two years for which data were available. The results of a paired samples t-test indicated that the imputation did not change the distribution of the data or group averages. Children in special education were excluded from analysis. The distribution of grades for children with three years of grades data is presented Table 7.

There was some variation in GPA across the three years of the study, and there were subtle differences between boys and girls. As shown in Table 8, GPA was the highest in Year 2, and the lowest in Year 3.

Table 7: Distribution of Grades (percentages)

Grade	GPA			3 Year GPA
	Year 1	Year 2	Year 3	
A (10.5 – 11.49)	9.6%	7.3%	4.1%	2.5%
A- (9.5 – 10.49)	11.2%	12.1%	11.6%	10.7%
B+ (8.5 – 9.49)	16.0%	22.6%	11.6%	16.5%
B (7.5 – 8.49)	16.8%	16.9%	20.7%	24.8%
B- (6.5 – 7.49)	17.6%	17.7%	15.7%	16.5%
C+ (5.5 – 6.49)	15.2%	12.9%	7.4%	14.0%
C (4.5 – 5.49)	9.6%	6.5%	9.9%	9.1%
C- (3.5 – 4.49)	1.6%	3.2%	8.3%	5.8%
D+ (2.5 – 3.49)	2.4%	0.8%	5.0%	0%
D (1.5 – 2.49)	0%	0%	2.5%	0%
D- (0.5 – 1.49)	0%	0%	2.5%	0%
F (<.49)	0%	0%	0.8%	0%

Throughout each of the three years, girls had slightly higher grades than boys, although, with the exception of Year 1, they were equivalent to the same letter grade (numerical and letter grades are presented to illustrate these differences). Girls had a higher three year GPA as well.

Table 8: Annual and Three Year Average Grade Point Average (GPA)

Children	GPA			3 Year GPA
	Year 1	Year 2	Year 3	
Sex				
Girls	B (7.86)	B (8.21)	B- (7.18)	B (7.73)
Boys	B- (7.47)	B (7.51)	B (6.63)	B- (7.07)
All children	B (7.68)	B (7.89)	B- (6.93)	B- (7.44)

Bivariate Analyses

Bivariate tests were used to examine relationships between language preference and GPA. These preliminary analyses were used to explore bivariate relationships among variables before testing the hypotheses.

Correlations

Bivariate analyses revealed significant associations between language preference and academic performance. Significant correlations using both Pearson r and Spearman's rho were found between three year GPA and the three different language preference measures, Primary, Binary and Composite Score. These are presented in Table 9. The two correlation measures yielded similar results, namely that preference for being spoken to in English is negatively correlated with academic performance, and bilingual preference is positively correlated with higher GPA. Bivariate correlations did not reveal any significant correlations between either measure of linguistic fit and academic performance.

T-test analyses of mean group differences in GPA

T-tests were used to examine three year GPA based on the binary independent variables sex, cohort and linguistic fit, as well as the binary measures of language preference. For analyses with each of these variables, Levene's test for equality of variance found no significant differences in the group variances, so the pooled variance estimate was used to calculate the t value.

Table 9: Language Preference and Three Year Grade Point Average (GPA)

	3 Year GPA	
Measure	Pearson Correlation	Spearman's rho
Primary Language Preference: Language in which child prefers to be spoken to (1=Spanish, 2=bilingual, 3=English)	-0.243 * (n=98)	-0.239 * (n=98)

Table 9 (Continued): Language Preference and Three Year Grade Point Average (GPA)

Measure	3 Year GPA	
	Pearson Correlation	Spearman's rho
Binary Language Preference: Prefers to be spoken to in English only	n/a	-0.212* (n=98)
Binary Language Preference: Prefers to be spoken to bilingually/ in both languages equally	n/a	0.212* (n=98)
Composite Score of Language Preference: Prefers to speak and be spoken to bilingually/ in both languages equally	.0240 * (n=98)	ns
Composite Score of Language Preference: Prefers to speak and be spoken to in English only	-0.278** (n=98)	-0.248 * n=98)

* = significant at .05 level
**=significant at .01 level
ns=not significant
n/a=not applicable

Although girls had a slightly higher three year GPA (mean=7.73 or B) compared to boys (mean=7.07 or B-), the results did not show the mean difference of 0.54 to be a significant difference in mean three year GPA based on sex.

When cohort was used to determine if there were any significant differences in three year GPA based on age, significant differences were found between younger and older children ($t_{(df=124)}$ =2.342; p< .05). Younger children had significantly higher three year average GPA (mean=7.84 or B) compared to older children (mean=7.10 or B-). The mean difference was 0.75. To determine if the cohort difference in average grades was present for both boys and girls, t-tests were run separately on boys and girls to examine possible differences in three year GPA based on age. However, these results revealed no significant mean differences among older and younger children when girls and boys were examined on independently.   T-tests also found no significant mean differences among boys and girls when cohorts were examined separately.

T-tests of three year GPA based on linguistic fit found no significant mean differences when all children were examined together and when girls and boys were examined separately.

Table 10: Mean Differences: Language Preference and Three Year Grade Point Average (GPA)

Measure	T	Df	Sig.	Mean difference	Std error difference
Binary Language Preference: Prefers to be spoken to in English Only	-2.296	96	0.024	-0.99	0.433

As bivariate correlations indicated that English only preference is negatively correlated with GPA and bilingual preference positively correlated with GPA, it raised the question of how English only and bilingual preference, as binary measures, might be related to GPA. Using the results of the correlations as baseline data, independent t-tests were conducted to understand if there were any significant differences in mean 3 year GPA among children using the Binary Language Preference measures. Significant mean differences in three year GPA were found based on a preference to be spoken to in English. The results are displayed in Table 10.

As indicated, for three year GPA children who preferred to be spoken to in English only (n=24) had significantly lower grades (mean =6.71 or B-) compared to children who did not prefer to be spoken to in English only (n=74) (mean=7.70 or B) when using the Binary Language Preference measure.

T-tests were also conducted to compare mean GPAs of students based on language preference for each year of the study. When looking at grades for each year individually, significant differences were found in year 2 only. In year 2, GPA for students who preferred their teacher teach in English had average grades that were lower and significantly different from those of children who did not prefer English instruction when using the Binary Language Preference measure. These results are displayed in Table 11 below.

Table 11: Mean Differences: Language Preference and Grade Point Average (GPA) for Year 2

Measure	t	Df	Sig	Mean difference	Std error difference
Binary Language Preference: Prefers teacher teach in English Only	-2.080	96	0.040	-0.75	0.358

The results of the t-test show that, although children with this English preference in Year 2 (n=51) had average mean grades (mean=7.51 or B) significantly below those of children who did not prefer their teacher teach in English (n=47) (mean=8.26) they were equivalent to the same letter grade (B).

ANOVA analyses of mean group differences in GPA

Both bivariate correlations and independent t-tests revealed significant correlations and mean group differences in GPA based on language preference as well as cohort. Although these indicated that English only preference was negatively correlated with GPA and bilingual preference positively correlated with GPA, these analyses were not sufficiently sophisticated to (1) examine differences among children with either a high, moderate or no preference for either English or bilingualism, and (2) examine differences among children based on their level of acculturation when using the Primary Language Preference measure. Thus, a one-way analysis of variance (ANOVA) was used to explore these differences and examine possible differences in 3 year GPA among children when using these three point measures of language preference.

Examination of the four Primary Language Preference variables did not yield any significant findings. However, significant mean group differences in 3 year GPA were found using the English and Bilingual Composite Score Language Preference measures.

For bilingual preference, children with no bilingual preference (n=11) had the lowest overall mean 3 year GPA (6.00 or C+), children with high bilingual preference (n=50) had the highest mean 3 year GPA (7.74 or B), and children with moderate bilingual preference (n=37) had a mean 3 year GPA just below children with high bilingual preference, although it was equivalent to the same letter grade (7.51 or B). The results of the ANOVA showed an overall significant difference in mean GPA between groups (F df=2, 95 = 4.118, p<.05). The Tukey HSD post hoc test was run to determine which groups were significantly different. Results of the Tukey test demonstrated that children with high bilingual preference had a significantly higher 3 year GPA compared to children with no bilingual preference (mean difference=1.74, p<.05). In addition, children with moderate bilingual preference had a significantly higher 3 year GPA compared to children with no bilingual preference (mean difference=1.51, p<.05) as well.

Similar results were found for English only preference. Children with high English only preference (n=10) had the lowest mean 3 year GPA (6 or C+), children with no English only preference (n=57) had the highest mean 3 year GPA (7.81 or B), and children with moderate English only preference (n=31) had a GPA in the middle (7.29 or B-). The results of the ANOVA showed an overall significant difference in mean GPA between groups (F df=2, 95 = 4.380, p<.05). As before, the Tukey HSD post hoc test was run to determine which groups were significantly different. Results of the Tukey test demonstrated that children with high English only preference had a significantly lower 3 year GPA compared to children with no bilingual preference (mean difference= -1.81, p<.05). No significant differences were found among children with moderate English only preference compared to children with no English only preference.

The results of the ANOVA and Tukey post hoc tests show that children with high and moderate bilingual preference had a significantly higher 3 year GPA (mean=7.74 and 7.51, respectively) compared to children with no bilingual preference (mean=6) when using the bilingual Composite Score of Language Preference. This finding was supported by test results using the English Composite Score of Language Preference which found that children with high

English only preference had a significantly lower GPA (mean=6) compared to children with no English only preference (mean=7.81). In terms of GPA, these results show that bilingual children perform better than English only monolingual children by almost one full letter grade, as they average a B over a C+.

ANOVA was also used to explore possible differences in 3 year GPA based on SES, the language spoken by the mother/in the home, the language the mother speaks with the child, and the language spoken in the school.

Tests of SES against three year GPA using ANOVA did not reveal any significant differences among children. In addition to SES, income was also examined to determine if there were significant differences in three year average based on income alone. However, no significant differences were found based on income either. Separate ANOVAs were run on boys and girls separately to examine possible differences in three year GPA based on either SES or income, but no significant differences were found.

To determine if there were any significant differences in three year average based on the language spoken by the mother/in the home, and the language spoken in the school, ANOVA tests of three year GPA were run based on the language the mother speaks, the language the mother speaks to the child, and the language the child speaks in school. However, no significant mean group differences in GPA were found when children were examined together or when boys and girls were examined separately.

In sum, the results of the t-tests and ANOVAs indicate significant mean group differences in three year GPA based on language preference and, to a much lesser degree, cohort. The results also indicate that there are no such significant differences based on sex, SES, linguistic fit, the language spoken by the mother/in the home, or the language spoken in the school.

The characteristics of children with different language preferences
To understand the characteristics of children with different language preferences, correlations were run using the English Binary Language Preference measures to determine if they might be similar or different from children with a bilingual preference. As shown in Table 12 below, there were a few significant correlations although they were all of a

small magnitude, indicating little more than some association. Because the language preference measures were binary, only the Spearman's rho correlation measure was used.

Table 12: Correlations: Children's Characteristics and English Preference

Characteristics	Prefers to speak English	Prefers to be spoken to in English	Prefers teacher teach in English	Prefers English for stories
Sex (boys)	0.012	0.182	0.245[*]	0.082
Age (older cohort)	0.139	-0.072	0.217[*]	-0.007
SES	0.156	0.011	0.039	0.082
School language (class type)				
Bilingual	-0.213[*]	0.073	-0.209[*]	-0.202[*]
English Only	0.120	-0.005	0.143	0.067
Transitioned	0.124	-0.095	0.086	0.187
Mother's / home language				
Mother speaks	-0.135	0.178	0.105	0.024
Mother speaks to	0.107	0.282[**]	0.179	0.247[*]
child	-			
Linguistic fit	0.193[*]	0.281[**]	-0.313[**]	0.065

* = significant at .05 level
**=significant at .01 level

The correlations above indicate that English preference is significantly correlated with a few factors, indicating that children who prefer English are somewhat different from those who prefer bilingualism along each of these independent variables. Specifically, sex, age, being in a bilingual class in school, the language the mother speaks to the child, and linguistic fit were variables along which children who preferred English differed from children who preferred bilingualism. SES and the language the mother speaks were not significantly correlated with language preference.

Preferring the teacher teach in English was positively correlated with being a boy, but girls and boys were not different based on the other three language preference measures. Being an older child was also positively correlated with preferring the teacher teach in English, indicating a difference between older and younger children based on this language preference measure only. These two results show there is some association between preferring the teacher teach in English and being an older child and being a boy.

Of the three different class types, being in a bilingual class for the three years of the study was negatively correlated with preferring to speak, have the teacher teach, and hear stories in, English. This indicates that children who preferred English in these areas but were in a bilingual class differed from children in bilingual education who preferred bilingualism. Conversely, preferring bilingualism for each of these four measures was positively associated with being in a bilingual class for the three years. Neither being in an English only class nor transitioning from a bilingual to an English only class was correlated with language preference. This shows, understandably, that there is a negative association between preferring English along three of the four measures, and being in a bilingual class.

The language the mother speaks to the child was positively correlated with the language in which the child prefers to be spoken to, and the language the child prefers to hear stories in. This shows that children who prefer English are somewhat different from children who prefer both languages based on the language their mother uses with them. The language the mother speaks with the child was a five point scaled measure, thus the mother speaking increasingly more English with the child is associated with children preferring to be spoken to and hear stories in English. Thus, children who prefer English are somewhat different from children who prefer bilingualism along these two measures, for whom there would be a negative association between language preference and the language the mother speaks.

Linguistic fit was negatively correlated with the language the child prefers to speak and the language s/he prefers the teacher teach in, and positively correlated with the language in which the child prefers to be spoken to. As linguistic fit was a binary measure where 1=some difference between the language preferred at home and at school, this indicates that some difference between home and school language preferences is positively associated with children preferring to be spoken to in English. However, it is negatively associated with children preferring to speak English or preferring the teacher teach in English. Thus, these results show that children who prefer English are somewhat different from children who prefer bilingualism along these three measures of language preference based on linguistic fit. It should be noted that these correlations may in part reflect associations with the measures that were used to create the measure linguistic fit.

Congruence between language at home and language at school
Linguistic congruence or dis-congruence between the home and the school could have an impact of children's academic performance. To explore this issue, a measure of linguistic fit was calculated. In addition, using the Primary Language Preference measures, a paired samples t-test was conducted to determine whether there was congruence or not between the languages the child prefers at home and the language the child prefers at school. There was no data on what language the child preferred to use with her/his parents. In which case the language the child prefers to be spoken to in was used as a proxy for home language preference, as the language children prefer to be spoken to in is likely the language children prefer their parents speak to them in.

Based on a three point coding scheme (1=Spanish, 2=bilingual, 3=English), the paired samples t-test found a significant difference between home (mean= 2.19) and school (mean=2.44) language preference ($t_{(df=104)}$= -3.353; p< .001). This result indicates a dis-congruence between the language children prefer to us at home and the language children prefer to use at school, meaning there is a lack of linguistic fit between the two contexts.

Multivariate Regression Analysis

Based on the results of the bivariate analyses, which found significant associations between language preference and GPA, as well as significant differences in GPA based on language preference, a multivariate regression analysis was conducted to estimate a model that best predicts academic achievement among children. Multivariate regression was used to test hypotheses 1 and 4:

H1: Children who are bilingual will have better levels of academic performance compared to children who are assimilated.

H4: Sex will moderate the way language preference relates to academic performance

A regression model was built using three year GPA as the dependent variable, and the Bilingual Composite Score of Language Preference as the independent variable of primary interest. Reflecting the results of the bivariate correlations, the regression modeling demonstrated that bilingual language preference, when controlling for sex, age, SES, and some interaction effects, is important in shaping academic outcomes. Linguistic fit between the home and the school had no significant predictive value on academic performance. These results are presented in Table 13.

The R-Squared for the full model is .25, indicating a high level of correlation between the dependent variable three year GPA, and all seven independent variables in the model. Thus, overall the model explains 25 percent of the variation in three year GPA. However, the Adjusted R-Squared indicates that the eight variables in the model account for just 18 percent of the variation in three year GPA.

Academic achievement is complex and influenced by many things, not all of which were captured in this model or examined through this research. Examining these factors would require a larger sample size and various additional measures not available in the CIDC data.

Evidently, other factors impact academic achievement for this group of children, or any children for that matter. However, in terms of whether or not language explains some of the variability in academic performance, this model clearly shows that these seven factors are significant predictors of academic performance, as indicated by the large and significant F-statistic for the full model (F=3.330, p< 01). With a beta of .467 (p<.001), bilingual preference emerged as a very strong predictor of three year GPA, accounting for 14 percent of the variation in GPA. Moreover, sex had a strong predictive value as well with a beta of .513 (p<.05). The estimate indicates there is a difference between boys and girls, namely that being a boy is positively predictive of academic performance. However, the significant interaction term between sex and bilingual preference (beta= -.760, p< .01), indicates a negative effect on GPA from the interaction between sex and bilingual language preference which together impact academic performance, when controlling for age, and SES.

Table 13: Multivariate Regression: Predictors of Academic Achievement

Factor	β	T	p
Sex	0.513	2.045	0.045
Cohort	-0.192	-1.362	0.178
SES	0.096	0.912	0.365
Bilingual Composite Score of Language Preference:	0.467	3.453	0.001
Interaction: sex X bilingual preference	-0.760	-3.135	0.003
Interaction: sex X age	-0.089	-0.492	0.624
Linguistic fit between the home and school (binary)	0.011	0.107	0.915

To explore possible gender differences, the regression model was run separately for boys and girls. As the first regression indicated that linguistic fit was not significantly correlated with GPA, it was removed from the model. The two interaction terms were removed as they were not applicable to this model. The results are presented in Table 14.

The results show a clear difference in the effect of bilingual preference on academic performance. Bilingual preference has a significant effect on girls' performance in school (beta=.483, p<.001) when controlling for SES and cohort. For boys, however, bilingual preference is not a significant predictor of GPA. For girls, the large and highly significant F-statistic for the full model (F=5.396, p< 01) indicates that these three variables are significant predictors of academic performance. The R-Squared indicates that 29 percent of the variation in three year GPA is explained by the model, which is very similar to the more conservative Adjusted R-Squared which indicates that these three variables alone explain 24 percent of the variation in three year GPA.

Table 14: Multivariate Regression: Bilingual Preference as a Predictor of Academic Achievement for Boys and Girls

Sex	β	T	p
Girls			
Cohort	-0.207	-1.527	0.135
SES	0.155	1.141	0.261
Bilingual Composite Score of Language			
Preference	0.483	3.611	0.001
Boys			
Cohort	-0.294	-1.713	0.097
SES	0.024	0.140	0.889
Bilingual Composite Score of Language			
Preference	-0.210	-1.223	0.231

These results indicate that girls with higher bilingual preference scores perform better in school. To determine whether English preference had a negative effect on the academic performance for girls or boys, separate regression models were run to examine the predictive value of English preference on academic achievement for boys and girls. These results are displayed in Table 15 below.

Consistent with the bilingual preference model, the regression for English preference indicates that language is a significant predictor of GPA for girls. With a beta of -.462 ($p<.001$), English preference was a significant predictor of GPA when controlling for SES and cohort, indicating that greater English only preference negatively impacts academic performance for girls. Although the model is small, the results for the girls are telling, as the large and highly significant F-statistic for the full model (F=4.916, $p< .01$) indicates that these three variables are significant predictors of academic performance. The R-Squared shows that 27 percent of the variation in GPA is explained by the three variables in the model, and the Adjusted R-Squared 22 percent.

In building the regression models, an attempt was made to fit measures of school engagement, such as how important the child thinks it is to get good grades or do homework (see Appendix A for measures), which could help explain academic performance and gender differences by examining them through another lens. However, none of these factors had any significant effects on boys, girls or the children as a whole. Furthermore, the sample size constrains the number of variables that can be put into either of the three models. In consideration of these limitations, the best models have been presented.

Table 15: Multivariate Regression Grouped by Sex: English Preference as a Predictor of Academic Achievement for Boys and Girls

Sex	β	t	P
Girls			
Cohort	-0.186	-1.355	0.183
SES	0.179	1.304	0.200
English Composite Score of			
Language Preference	-0.462	-3.418	0.001
Boys			
Cohort	-0.311	-1.792	0.083
SES	0.032	0.186	0.853
English Composite Score of			
Language Preference	0.175	1.009	0.321

The results of the regression analyses clearly indicate that language preference impacts academic performance girls and boys differently. This indicates that sex is a moderator between language preference and academic performance, as it changes the way the two relate to each other. Although the regression model including all children revealed that language preference has significant predictive value for academic performance, upon further analysis it became clear that this result was driven by the girls in the sample alone. For girls, bilingual or English preference each predict approximately one quarter of the variation in academic performance. However, for boys, language cannot explain any of the variation in GPA.

In sum, the results of the multivariate analysis indicate the positive returns of bilingual preference, and the negative returns of English preference, to academic performance. Specifically, bilingual preference was found to be positively correlated with three year GPA, and English preference negatively correlated with three year GPA. In addition, the regression analysis showed that greater bilingual preference is positively predictive of academic performance, and greater English preference negatively predictive. However, these results held for the girls and not the boys: the regression analysis revealed that language preference does not have any explanatory power for the boys in the sample. Thus, as regard to hypotheses 1, the results show that girls with bilingual preference have better academic outcomes compared to girls who are preferred English only, as girls who prefer English have lower levels of academic performance compared to children with a bilingual preference.

Longitudinal Analysis

The longitudinal analysis explored possible time trends and to determine if language can predict academic performance for each of the three years of the study. Like the preceding regression analysis, the longitudinal analysis tested hypotheses 1 and 4.

The results thus far show that language was significantly correlated with academic performance, and could predict some of the variation in three year GPA for girls. However, the regression analysis did could not determine whether there were differences in academic performance over the three years of the study when controlling for time or if language preference could explain changes in academic performance from years 1 to 3. However, because the data did not include longitudinal measures of language preference it was not possible to examine if child language preference changed over time and whether these changes impacted academic performance. (Measures of language preference were only available for year 2 of the study.)

The panel data modeling sought to understand the impact of language preference over the three years of the study. The composite score of bilingual language preference measure was modeled with repeated measures of individual GPA for each of the three years. A mixed model with both fixed and random effects was built for the longitudinal analysis. The random effects were the subjects themselves, and the fixed effects were the variables of interest (language preference, sex, cohort, SES). The purpose of this analysis was to estimate the fixed effects for the variables of interest. Including the subjects as a random effect helped the model explore the variation in GPA over the three years by correlating the results in individual subjects. The model generated an estimate for Year 1, Year 2 and Year 3 which indicates the average GPA for all children in the model for each year. By adjusting for the effects of each year of the study, the model was then able to estimate the fixed effects for each variable of interest, most importantly bilingual language preference and sex, on average over the three years. In generating the estimates the model set one parameter for each variable to zero, and that parameter was used as the reference group for the others in that group. Thus, the estimates generated indicate how much better or worse individual children are performing relative to the reference group. For example, in Table 14, boys have a letter "a" indicating they are the reference group, whereas girls have an estimate. Since the estimate for the girls is positive and significant, this indicates that girls, on average, will perform that much better each year compared to the boys.

The ability to model GPA for the three years was a big departure from the regression modeling and is different from the structural equation modeling (to be described in the next section). This analysis required a new dataset of the panel data consisting of three cases, one for each year, for each of the children in the study, which had the effect of tripling the sample size. It is important to note that the larger sample size lent more power to the longitudinal model. The results of the best model fit to the data are presented Table 16. Linguistic fit was not a good fit for the linear mixed model and was not included.

Supporting the results of the regression analysis, this model shows that bilingual language preference, when interacting with sex, does predict GPA for each year when adjusting for the effects of each year and when controlling for SES. The results also show that cohort is significantly positively predictive of GPA over the three years; specifically that younger children perform better on average compared to the older children. Most interestingly, however, is that the estimates indicate that the effects of bilingual preference for girls and boys are moving in the opposite direction. For girls, the beta for no bilingual preference (beta= -2.6, p< .001) indicates a significant negative effect on GPA compared to girls with high bilingual preference, as does the beta for moderate bilingual preference (beta= -0.9, p< .05). However, the results show that the opposite is true for boys, for whom high bilingual preference has a significantly positive effect (beta= 1.5, p<.05) compared to boys with high bilingual preference. However, the results of moderate bilingual preference for boys were not significant.

Table 16: Predictive Value of Bilingual Language Preference over Three Years

Factor	B	T	p
Interaction:			
girls X no bilingual preference	-2.618501	-4.892	0.000
Interaction:			
girls X moderate bilingual preference	-0.910759	-2.417	0.016
Interaction:			
girls and high bilingual preference	a	n/a	n/a
Interaction:			
boys X no bilingual preference	1.531294	2.405	0.017
Interaction:			
boys X moderate bilingual preference	0.121650	0.288	0.774
Interaction:			
boys and high bilingual preference	a	n/a	n/a
Sex			
Girls	1.512591	3.947	0.000
Boys	a	n/a	n/a
Elementary age			
Lower (younger cohort)	0.876916	3.281	0.001
Upper (older cohort)	a	n/a	n/a
SES	0.102796	1.456	.147
Year 1	0.947520	3.005	0.003
Year 2	0.882585	2.799	0.006
Year 3	a	n/a	n/a

a=Parameter is set to 0, thus an estimate is not generated

Because the results indicate a gender difference, separate mixed models of bilingual preference were built for boys and girls so they could be examined separately. As indicated in Table 17, these results tease out some of the subtleties of the preceding model, which show gender differences that are consistent with the results of the regression models.

These results show some interesting distinction between boys and girls that further explain some of the results of the whole group model.

Table 17: Predictive Value of Bilingual Language Preference over Three Years, by Sex

Sex	β	T	P
Girls			
No bilingual preference	-2.597691	-5.076	0.000
Moderate bilingual preference	-0.886755	-2.450	0.016
High bilingual preference	a	n/a	n/a
Younger cohort (grades 1-3)	0.651345	1.916	0.058
SES	1.288990	1.447	0.151
Year 1	0.605226	1.503	0.135
Year 2	0.837785	2.081	0.040
Year 3	a	n/a	n/a
Boys			
No bilingual preference	1.571218	2.320	0.022
Moderate bilingual preference	0.126243	.273	0.786
High bilingual preference	a	n/a	n/a
SES	0.064406	0.563	0.575
Younger cohort (grades 1-3)	1.170131	2.731	0.008
Year 1	1.382353	2.748	0.007
Year 2	0.941176	1.871	0.064
Year 3	a	n/a	n/a

a=Parameter is set to 0, thus an estimate is not generated

For girls, no bilingual preference (beta= -2.6, p< .001) and moderate bilingual preference (beta= -0.9, p< .05) are both significantly negatively predictive of GPA compared to girls with high bilingual preference.

For boys, there is some evidence of an opposite effect, as no bilingual preference (beta= 1.6, p< .05) was significantly positively predictive of three year GPA (p<.01) compared to boys with high bilingual preference. However, moderate bilingual preference had no significant effect for the boys. These results suggest that boys who prefer English do better than those who do not. In addition to bilingual preference, these results indicate a cohort effect for boys (p<.01) which was not found for the girls. This indicates that younger boys perform better on average compared to older boys. The gender differences for the effects of cohort also suggest that the cohort effect found in the model with all children was primarily driven by the boys.

These results indicate that sex and bilingual preference can predict GPA for each year when adjusting for time and controlling for SES and cohort. These results echo the gender differences found in the regression modeling, although the longitudinal analysis found that bilingual preference effects girls and boys in opposite ways. These results offer another dimension that helps to explain the effects of language preference on academic performance over the three years, and improves upon the regression modeling by controlling for time. However, the results require fine tuning. To better understand the nuances of these results requires the use of more complex measures, which was achieved through the structural equation modeling.

Structural Equation Modeling

The structural equation modeling examined associations among observed and latent variables by exploring more complex measures of language and academic performance, as well as models of the associations between language in different contexts and academic performance. Specifically, the structural equation modeling sought to examine possible associations among the language of the child, the mother/home, and the school, as well as the hypothesized effects of each of these latent constructs on academic performance. The structural equation modeling was conducted to test hypotheses 1, 2, 3 and 4.

H1: Children who are bilingual will have better levels of academic performance compared to children who are assimilated.
H2. The language spoken by the mother/in the home will have a direct effect on academic performance.
H3: The language spoken in school will have a direct effect on academic performance.
H4: Sex will moderate the way language preference relates to academic performance

Developing the measurement models
García Coll and Marks (2009) have confirmed a good fit for measuring academic performance as presented below in Figure 2. The construct

presented was measured by using GPA for each year of the three years, and the teacher's rating of the child in year three.

Figure 2: Latent variable: Academic Performance

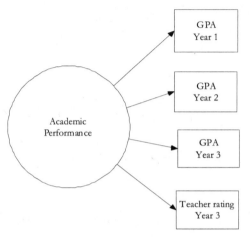

(*Notes:* model fit statistics: Chi Square=.81, p=.37; CFI=1.00; NFI=.99; RMSEA=0.00)

The construct academic performance has a perfect measurement fit as determined by all four of the model fit statistics.

The measurement model for child language preference was the first construct fit for this research. The observed variables that produced a successfully fitted model were all four of the Bilingual Binary Language Preference variables. The measurement model of child bilingual preference in Figure 3 below has a perfect measurement fit as determined by three of the four fit statistics of model fit. One of these measures, RMSEA, is high, but it is just below the highest measure acceptable (Gefen et al, 2000).

To contrast the child bilingual preference model, and attempt was made to fit a measurement model of child English preference. However, even with the variety of language preference variables available, it was not possible to build this latent variable. That it was not possible to fit this model suggests that either the indicators available are insufficient to capture this construct or that the measures themselves are poor. Most importantly, although the results of some of the previous analyses indicate that English preference is negatively correlated with GPA and negatively predictive of GPA in the long-term, the inability to build this model could indicate that English preference is a weak construct that in and of itself does not hold much value for this group of children. This would suggest that bilingual preference or not preferring English only, as opposed to English preference, is the factor of importance when trying to understand this sample of children.

Figure 3: Latent variable: Child Bilingual Preference

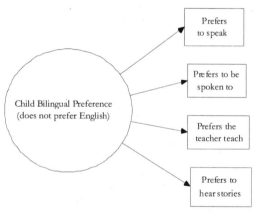

(*Notes:* model fit statistics: Chi Square=3.62, p=.16; CFI=.95; NFI=.91; RMSEA=.08)

In addition to child language preference, a measurement model was built for the child's home language. In building this measurement model, the measures that were successfully fit were the indicators of the mother's language use and the mother's language comfort. Given that such a large percentage of children were growing up in single female headed households, it is understandable why these indicators were the best fit for this construct. The construct was measured by using the questions what language/s the mother speaks, what language the mother speaks to the child, and the four scaled indicators of the mother's language comfort. The measurement model of mother's language use and comfort in Figure 4 below has a perfect measurement fit as determined by four fit statistics of model fit.

Figure 4: Latent variable: Mother's Language use and Comfort

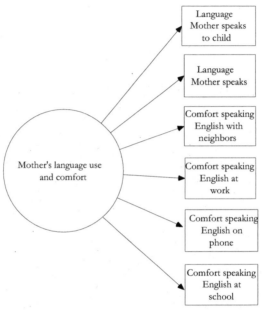

(Notes: model fit statistics: Chi Square=11.86, p=.22; CFI=.99; NFI=.96; RMSEA=.05)

Efforts were made to specify a measurement model of the language spoken in the school, but it was not possible to build this latent variable. The indicators that were used in this effort were the number of bilingual and Latino students in the school for each of the three years, and the scaled question whether or not the teacher thinks children do better in school if they come from families that speak English regularly (from the teacher questionnaire). That it was not possible to fit this model indicates that either the indicators were insufficient to fit this construct, or that the measures themselves are poor. Therefore, it was not possible to explore whether the language spoken in the school has direct or indirect effects on academic performance.

Fitting the Structural Equation Model

Once the latent constructs for academic achievement, child language, and mother's language were specified, the next step entailed attempting to fit the structural equation model with the three latent variables while controlling for SES, sex, and age. Each latent variable is a successfully fitted measure of a complex construct. Thus, it is important to note that once the latent variables have been specified it is not possible to adjust them in any way by adding or removing variables. Therefore, fitting the structural equation model requires using the specified latent variables as they are, although attempting to fit additional observed variables, such as controls, into the model as stand-alone variables can be part of the process of building the structural equation model.

Fitting a structural model using child language and academic performance was successful. However, attempting to fit mother's language into the model was not successful as it destabilized the entire model. Thus, efforts to fit a structural equation model to examine associations between language and academic performance were not successful with both latent measures of child's language and mother's language in the model, with or without the inclusion of the stand alone observed variable SES, sex, age, and linguistic fit between the home and the school. From this point, attempts were made to fit separate models to examine (1) associations between the mother's language and academic performance with child language removed from the model, and (2) associations between child language and mother's language with academic performance removed from the model. However, it was not possible to successfully fit either of these models. This shows that there was no significant association between mother's language and the child's academic performance with or without the inclusion of additional controls variables. Similarly, there was no significant association between child language and mother's language. Therefore, it was not possible to determine if the mother's language has a direct or indirect effect on academic performance.

Given that the latent variable mother's language could not be fit into a structural model, efforts were made to fit the observed measures used to build the latent variable mother's language into the structural model as stand-alone variables one at a time, along with the latent variable child's language. These efforts, however, did not result in a successfully fitted model either. Additional efforts were also made to include the observed measures of school language as stand-alone variables in the model one at a time as well, but these attempts were also not successful. Thus, the successfully fitted structural equation model did not include any measures of mother's or school language. Although the model controlled for sex, it was not possible to successfully fit a structural equation model that controlled for SES, cohort, and enrollment in special education as well. It was, however, possible to fit this model by excluding children in enrolled in special education at any point during the three years, thus the final model controls for enrollment in special education by excluding those children from the model. The structural equation model is presented in Figure 5.

The model fit statistics point to a borderline successfully fitted model. The CFI indicates good model fit, although the NFI is just shy of .09, however the NFI may underestimate fit for a small sample size and therefore the more liberal cutoff of .08 is sometimes used to determine model fit; RMSEA is over .06, although it is acceptable up to .08 (Gefen et al, 2000). The Chi Square, however, is far below .05. However, the Chi Square as a measure reflects combinations of variables and cases in the data, and is therefore sensitive to both sample size and the number of variables in the model. Thus, the interplay of these two factors can throw off the model as reflected in a small Chi Square, and may not necessarily reflect a weak association between bilingualism and academic performance. For this reason additional fit statistics are provided in addition to the Chi Square.

The successfully fitted model of child's bilingual preference and academic achievement shows that bilingual preference can explain some of the variability in academic performance. Specifically, this means that child's bilingual preference is significantly positively associated with academic achievement ($p<.05$) when controlling for sex. However, the estimates show that sex is significantly associated academic performance. Specifically, being a boy is negatively associated with academic performance when it works through bilingual language preference as a mediator. The notion that bilingual language preference mediates the effects of sex on academic performance is somewhat perplexing. However, if sex captures certain behavioral factors and therefore could be, for example, a proxy for school engagement, this result could indicate that motivation and school values could perhaps explain some of the variation in academic performance, as opposed to sex itself, or bilingual preference for that matter. To rule out this possibility, two models were run by replacing sex with a measure of school engagement (see Appendix A for indicators). However, it was not possible to fit such a model, suggesting that there might be differences between boys and girls where associations between language preference and academic performance could have different implications for children along gender lines. This would reflect some of the findings of both the OLS regression and longitudinal models, which found differences between boys and girls. In building the previous models, teasing out some of these differences entailed examining both groups separately. Therefore, an attempt was made to fit separate structural models for the girls and boys.

Figure 5: Final Structural Equation Model: Child Bilingual Preference and Academic Performance

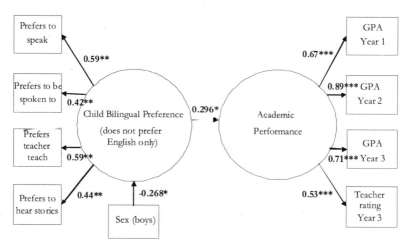

(*Notes:* model fit statistics: Chi Square=40.80, p=.02; CFI=.92; NFI=.83; RMSEA=.07. Path coefficients are standardized and significant: *= p<.05, **= p<.01, ***=p<.001)

Fitting a structural model for the girls to examine the association between girl's bilingual preference and academic achievement was successful when controlling for SES, although it was not possible to fit a successful model when controlling for age and/or linguistic fit between the home and the school. When the girls are examined separately from the boys the sample becomes very small, which in SEM prohibits building more variables into the model. The final structural equation model for the girls is presented in Figure 6.

Three out of the four statistics of model fit indicate a successfully fitted mode. Although the NFI is just under .9, the Chi Square, CFI and RMSEA show indicate that this is strong model fit for the girls. The estimates for this model indicate a much more significant positive association ($p<.01$) between bilingual preference and academic achievement that emerges for the girls once the boys are removed from the model, and when controlling for SES, which has no statistically significant association with academic performance.

Figure 6: Final Structural Equation Model: Girls' Bilingual Preference and Academic Performance.

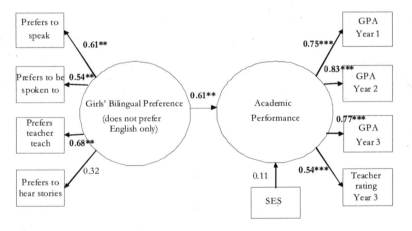

(*Notes:* model fit statistics: Chi Square=28.29, p=.29; CFI=.97; NFI=.84; RMSEA=.04. Path coefficients are standardized and significant: **= $p<.01$, ***=$p<.001$)

The results of the girls specific model suggest that the results of the structural model fitted for all children are driven by the association between bilingual preference and academic achievement for girls alone, which masked the absence of a similar association for the boys by having boys and girls in the model together and controlling for sex instead of examining both groups separately on their own terms.

Although it was possible to model bilingualism and academic achievement for the girls, it was not possible to successfully fit an equivalent model for the boys. In light of these results, to examine whether English preference could be a suitable construct for the boys, an effort to build such a measurement model for the boys only, was attempted. Unlike the unsuccessful attempt to fit a measurement model of English preference for all the children, a model of English preference for the boys was successfully fit when using the four English Binary Language Preference measures. However, attempts to build a structural equation model for the boys with this latent variable were not successful. This indicates that although English preference is a latent variable that holds for the boys and can stand on its own, it is not a construct that is associated with academic performance and, in the context of this study, has no discernible meaning.

Limitations

This research allowed for the close examination of language and academic performance as regards a particular group of children. Although various complementary statistical models were built, which together offer detailed and nuanced evidence that provides a thorough and comprehensive understanding of these children, there are limitations to this research.

Sample size presents one of the key limitations of this research. As the sample size was small, it limited the number of variables that could be fit into the models. Furthermore, although missing data was handled using standard data imputation techniques, case deletion, and estimation methods for missing data, missing data does pose some limitations. Another limitation is that the measures of language used were self reported measures of language preference. Although the interview data is rich, response bias may be an issue, as the children and parents may have reported what they thought they should say or what they felt the interviewer wanted to hear. Furthermore, longitudinal measures of language preference were not available, thus it was not possible to examine if child language changes over time or if such changes are associated with academic performance. Additionally, as the indicators used were measures of language preference, this research cannot determine if and to what extent language proficiency can explain some of the variation in academic performance. Likewise, this research did not have IQ or such similar data, and thus was not able to determine if the impact of language on academic performance are the result of differences in intelligence as opposed to language preference. Similarly, it was not possible to determine if the mother's language has any impact on either child language or academic performance. In addition, although this research found associations and determined the predictive value of language on academic performance, these results cannot show causation. Lastly, as this research was focused on understanding one particular group of children, the results are not generalizeable to any other population.

Summary

The purpose of this research was to understand the impact of language on academic outcomes, specifically, if language acculturation could explain some of the variation in academic performance for children of immigrant families from the Dominican Republic. Four analytic approaches were used to explore this question, bivariate analyses, multivariate regression analysis, a longitudinal analysis, and the structural equation modeling. The analyses resulted in three primary models of the relationship between language and academic performance: a multivariate regression models, linear mixed models that controlled for the effects of time, and structural equation models. These three complementary models supplement each other and serve to tell a thorough story of the impact of language on academic performance at one moment in time, over the three years of the study, and through the use of more complex measures than those afforded in regression and mixed linear modeling.

In terms of whether acculturation impacts academic performance, the short answer is that it does. Bilingual preference among children is significantly positively correlated with GPA, whereas English preference is negatively correlated. Although bilingual preference was found to be significantly predictive of three year GPA, the results indicate that this is the case for girls and not boys, for whom language preference had little to no explanatory power. Thus, sex is clearly moderating the effects of language preference on academic performance. In the longitudinal model, bilingual preference was found to be strongly predictive of three year average for girls when controlling for time. For boys, however, the results indicate that no bilingual preference is positively predictive of academic performance over the three years, which is different from the results of the regression modeling. Thus, the results for boys are mixed.

The final structural equation modeling helped to further explain the relationship between language and academic performance through the use of more complex measures. Although it was not possible to determine if the mother's language or the language spoken in school have a direct or indirect effect on academic performance or on child language preference, the modeling did show a significant association between bilingual preference and academic performance, a very strong association for girls, but virtually no association for boys. The results of the structural equation modeling indicate that language can explain some of the variation in overall academic performance for girls. For boys, however, the results suggest that language does not have a significant impact on academic performance.

In sum, the results provide evidence of the educational immigrant paradox for girls, but not for boys. The underlying hypotheses of this research, that there are benefits associated with bilingualism and risks that come with English monolingualism for children of immigrant families, were supported for girls, although language preference of any kind was found to have little explanatory power for boys. These results will be discussed in the next chapter, along with the policy implications of the study findings and recommendations for future research.

CHAPTER 7
So what does all this Mean?

This research explored whether evidence of the educational immigrant paradox could be identified in middle childhood. To that end, it tested whether child language preference impacts academic performance, as well as if the different contexts of children's lives affect academic achievement. This research was designed to answer the question, Can language acculturation explain some of the variation in academic performance for children of immigrant families from the Dominican Republic? This study focused on exploring this question for a sample of children in middle childhood, an age group that has been understudied and about whom culturally specific, in-depth research on children of immigrant families is lacking. This research was based on the premise that bilingualism is a cultural and developmental asset, and conducted within an ecological framework that sought to consider the environmental aspects and contextual factors that characterize children's lives. With this as a foundation, this research examined the following four hypotheses:

H1. Children who are bilingual will have better levels of academic performance compared to children who are assimilated.

H2. The language spoken by the mother/in the home will have a direct effect on academic performance.

H3: The language spoken in school will have a direct effect on academic performance.

H4: Sex will moderate the way language preference relates to academic performance

As regards hypothesis 1, the central component of this research, this study found that girls with bilingual preference had higher levels of academic performance than girls who preferred English. Similarly, but to a lesser degree, the findings indicate that girls who preferred English had lower levels of academic performance than those who preferred bilingualism. With regard to hypothesis 2, an association between the language spoken by the mother/in the home and academic performance was not found, thus neither a direct or indirect effect of mother's/home language on academic performance was identified. Regarding hypotheses 3, a latent construct for the language spoken in the school could not be fit. Thus, it was not possible to explore whether the language spoken in the school had direct or indirect effects on academic performance as an association between school language and academic performance was not identified. That it was not possible to fit this model suggests the indicators used to capture this construct were inadequate. With regard to hypothesis 4, sex emerged as a key explanatory factor for understanding language preference and academic performance as it moderated the relationship between the two.

Findings overall

This research found that language preference was strongly predictive of academic performance for Dominican girls, but had little explanatory power for Dominican boys. Additionally, it was not possible to specify an association between mother's language and the language spoken in the school, on either child language or academic achievement. These results raise three important questions: (1) what can explain the connection between academic achievement and language preference, (2) what could explain the different results for boys and girls, and (3) what other factors could, theoretically, explain academic achievement among Dominican boys? This chapter will discuss the empirical findings and alternative explanations for the different results for boys and girls. These findings will be discussed in light of the familial and socio-cultural context in which the children are embedded.

Issues for girls

The key finding from this research is that bilingual preference is predictive of higher levels of academic performance for girls. This is consistent with research that has found that adolescents who are fluent in English and the home language do better than those who do not speak English or are limited English proficient (Fernandez & Nielsen, 1986, Portes & Rumbaut, 2001; Rumberger & Larson, 1998; Stanton-Salazar & Dornbusch, 1995; Suarez-Orozoco & Suarez-Orozoco, 1995). The study shows that, for girls, bilingual preference is a successful acculturation strategy that is associated with higher levels of academic performance. The positive effects of bilingualism have been found for adolescents, and this research adds to the literature by finding evidence of this among children in middle childhood. The study results are consistent with the empirical and theoretical literature, and suggest that being able to successfully manage both the home language/culture and the dominant/school language/culture (bilingualism/biculturalism) can nurture success among children of immigrants. This reflects research findings which have found that distance between children and their parents' immigrant culture and language negatively affects educational outcomes (Portes and Zhou, 1993; Kao & Tienda, 1995; Rumbaut, 1995, Suarez-Orozco & Suarez-Orozco, 1995).

The results for girls suggest that bilingualism is a resource and may indicate the risks that accompany English monolingualism. The findings confirm the underlying premise of this research that bilingualism is an asset- not a liability- that allows children to bridge two distinct worlds, those of the home and school, which, for this sample of children, are quite different. Dominicans in Providence are part of larger, well established and strongly interconnected pan-ethnic Latino community that shares Spanish as their common language. The children in this research are binational, as the Dominican community in Providence "is defined by its multiple social, economic, and familial links to the Dominican Republic. These links are maintained by a regular bi-directional flow of goods, ideas, and people and through the daily reproduction of linguistic and cultural practices from the island" (Bailey, 2002, p.33).

Because the cultural ties within the community are amplified by the strong bonds and networks that span both countries, the need for Dominican and Spanish cultural and linguistic tools and resources is obvious. "The vitality of this community... connects young Dominicans to their parents' language, culture, and history" (Bailey, 2000, p.9). Clearly, a grasp of Spanish is a requisite for nurturing strong and healthy family, community and cultural ties. As the children live and attend school in the US, the need for English language skills goes without explanation. Thus, perhaps bilingualism helps the girls balance their dual and competing roles as Dominicans and Americans; hence the reasons why it would be associated with better performance in school.

Although this research did not prove empirically an association between home language and academic performance, theoretically the strong association between girls bilingual preference and academic achievement could be interpreted as evidence of effectively acculturated and successfully adapted children for whom bilingual preference provides the tools to successfully participate in both the home and school cultures. Theoretically, bilingual preference could indicate a role as a "bridge-walker," children who function as cultural negotiators who can effectively serve as cultural and linguistic bridges between the home and the school with a positive impact on their own wellbeing, as evidenced by their better academic outcomes. Furthermore, maintenance of the home language could indicate strong relationships with their parents (or at least stronger relationships than would be the case if parents and children did not speak the same language), which might lead to greater parent/family support in their education.

Language is a form of communication, and if children and their parents are effectively and comfortably able to communicate with each other, parents are more likely to ask about school, talk to their child's teacher, help with homework, and might have a greater capacity to support education in the home. If children can talk to their parents, they are more likely to talk about school and share what they are learning, talk about difficulties they are having, ask questions, say when they do not understand something and ask for help. Parents who can communicate with their children might thus be more involved in their child's education. All these things nurture the learning process and promote a greater understanding of content area skills and concepts through an interactive and supportive process. Furthermore, language is the vehicle by which knowledge and values are transmitted, so children who speak their parents' language might be more likely to understand and internalize their parent's feelings about the importance of an education, the need to do well in school, and the expectations of them.

Issues regarding the family and mother's language

This research could not identify a measurable effect of home language on academic performance- what might that mean? The CIDC data offered a unique opportunity to examine a specific group of children very closely. However, the sample recruited may reflect self-selection resulting from the study's design. Although the sampling technique has clear advantages, it could have resulted in little variability among the study's participants, which is needed for analytic purposes. The children shared similar demographic and socioeconomic characteristics, thus the purposeful sampling technique had the dis/advantageous effect of essentially controlling for factors such as socioeconomic status. Thus the homogeneity of the sample could explain why an effect was not identified.

However, girls' language preference had a strong association with academic performance. This would be consistent with ecological theory which holds that factors more proximal to the child (her/his individual language preference) should be more highly correlated with performance than those that are more distal. Thus, the association between girls' language preference and academic achievement might be so strong as to make it impossible to see any associations between mother's/home language and academic performance as it is a more distal process.

Alternatively, given that no association was found with mother's language, consideration should be given to what language between children and parents might represent. Although language, literally, defines the mode of communication, in practice it reflects more than just the kind of words that are exchanged, devoid of any meaning. Thus, it may not be parent/family language itself that has a positive or negative effect, but, as discussed, what a language means and what linguistic dis/congruence affords or denies that impacts children. Therefore, in retrospect, separating language acculturation from overall psychological acculturation (which includes behaviors, feelings and many other aspects and socio-cultural dimensions beyond the scope of this study) may have made it difficult, if not impossible, to identify interactions between parents and children with regard to language. This study was not focused on the totality of dimensions that characterize acculturation, but rather linguistic acculturation only, and it may not be possible to tease out the impact of parent/family language acculturation without a larger examination of the more complex process of acculturation and its tangential behaviors, parenting and cultural practices, within which language acculturation occurs. Perhaps language is one of several factors that need to be considered together.

Issues for boys

This study affirms the need for culturally-specific research that examines groups closely on their own terms, as opposed to comparative studies that could mask the nuances that characterize distinct groups (Phinney & Landin, 1998). It points to different stories for girls and boys regarding the influence of language preference on academic achievement. What is it about the boys in this study that distinguish them from the girls, as evident in the absence of a similar effect of language preference on academic performance? A large number of the children were being raised by single mothers, and the absence of a father or male role model could be detrimental to growing boys at a formative developmental stage, especially given that the families were primarily poor/low income and the mother's had low levels of education. Without a male role model, the images and models available to boys are those in the extended family and community, but also, importantly, those prevalent in the media and popular culture. Given that the children in this study are children of color, the possible consequences of this are exacerbated by the children's minority status.

Dominicans are not racially white, in the US sense, as over 85 percent of Dominicans are of African ancestry (Bailey, 2002). Thus, more often than not, Dominicans will be raced black in the US. Thus, they will contend with the issues faced by the Latino population as well as many of those faced by the Black population, namely racism. Dominican boys will thus struggle against many of the same issues as black boys, such as stereotypes and barriers based on race, in addition to those faced by Latino boys and the myriad issues of acculturation they must reconcile as children of immigrant families. How do Dominican boys, as black males, fit into the US socio-cultural and racial landscape? How does their race characterize, perhaps define, their experience? There are powerful stereotypes and negative models of behavior and achievement about black people in this country, models that are different for girls and boys, men and women. The stereotypes of black men and women, and Latino men and women, are grossly different, as are the social issues that distinguish the experiences of males and females of color. What does it mean to be growing up an urban, black, Latino male in the US? What does society communicate to young black boys? There is a strong message about black men and boys which says that black males are criminals, gang members, drug dealers, violent, and dangerous, if they are not professional athletes. Certainly it is a message that does not emphasize black men as high achievers. The landmark studies by Clark and Clark in the 1940s, using dolls to measure the effects of racism on young black children, showed the profound negative effects that stereotypes have on black children at a young age (Clark & Clark, 1939, 1940, 1974). These findings have since been replicated, and bolstered by studies of stereotype threat which found that repeated exposure to negative stereotypes, particularly those faced by minority students in academic settings, can negatively affect the extent to which that domain is valued, which can have a negative effect on outcomes (Steele, 1997; Steele & Aronson, 1995). Clearly, these stereotypes, expectations, and pressures can have a negative effect on children at a very young age. The consequences of our racial problems are perhaps best summarized by Professor Carola Suarez-Orozco in testimony prepared for a hearing of the US House of Representatives: "A climate of racial profiling and discrimination has negative implications for acculturation, social belongingness, and the civic engagement of the next generation of immigrant youth. Being the subject of such divisive stereotyping is likely to further inequality and lead to numerous adverse cognitive, affective, motivational, and behavioral effects that are well documented" (Suarez-Orozco, 2010).

There are vicious stereotypes and negative and racist images of girls and women of color prevalent in society as well, such as that "they" are lazy, welfare queens, or sex objects, however, there is a qualitative difference between the message conveyed to boys and that delivered to girls. Thus, the implications and consequences of our profound racial problems and the messages they carry are different, in some ways, for boys, and may be a cause of their low levels of academic achievement compared to girls. The gender gap in education has been documented as girls (of all races/ethnicities) perform better academically than boys in elementary school through college. In short, girls of color do better in school than boys of color, and this study and others (Lopez, et al., 2002) have found that girls of immigrant families have higher GPAs than boys of the same immigrant group.

Men and boys of color, black men and boys in particular, are being left behind in a way that girls are not, in a way that is distinctly connected to matters of race/ethnicity. Perhaps these realities can help explain why language preference alone does not hold much explanatory power for Dominican boys, as clearly race together with gender have profound effects on academic performance. Racism and our inequalities and inequities present certain challenges and afford or deny things to people on the basis of race, and in particular race as it interacts with gender. Perhaps language is tied to factors for boys that are less of an issue for girls. Thus, the key factors that might help explain how acculturation unfolds and impacts academic performance may be different for boys and girls

In retrospect, perhaps trying to understand the impact of language acculturation alone on academic achievement is not an appropriate approach for boys. Perhaps language acculturation was too narrow a construct, as it did not capture the multidimensionality of acculturation and the experiences it defines for individuals, namely boys, for whom the factors that characterize acculturation and impact academic performance might be more complicated. Perhaps a better model for boys would be one that seeks to understand the acculturation of Dominican boys at the intersection of race and culture/language, to understand the different ways they might be acculturating and the different places they might be acculturating to. This would be consistent with the proposition that acculturation is not a uniform or linear process, and that immigrants and their children adjust to life in the US using different strategies and following different paths. As Portes & Rumbaut (2001) state, "the process [of acculturation] is subject to too many contingencies and affected by too many variables to render the image of a relatively uniform and straightforward path credible. Instead, the present second generation is better defined as undergoing a process of *segmented assimilation* where outcomes vary across immigrant minorities and where rapid integration and acceptance into the American mainstream represent just one possible solution." (p.45). It would appear that something different is happening with Dominican girls and boys as regards acculturation. Although it cannot be determined from the data available for this research, perhaps the boys are acculturating to a different segment of society than the girls, and maybe the fact that language cannot explain some of the variation in academic performance for boys is an early indication of that. Perhaps race can explain academic performance in a way that language cannot.

Gender, bilingual preference, and academic performance

The striking difference in the effects of bilingual preference between girls and boys might reflect the different ways girls and boys are socialized within the family. Gender based expectations and standards of behavior are engrained in cultures throughout the Americas, where gender roles run deep. This is especially evident in the organization and central role of the family. Diverse peoples in Latin America possess the distinct cultural value of *familismo*. *Familismo* constitutes strong identification with and attachment to the family, where pride, solidarity, loyalty, and obligation to the family, are paramount. However, *familismo* values different things for males and females and thus places different but complementary gender-based pressures and expectations on people; in particular girls are reared to become caregivers whereas boys are reared to become providers.

As much as the children are acculturating to life in the US, they are also being enculturated into their Dominican culture. Throughout the world, more often than not, children are socialized and parented in ways that are based on gender. In the Dominican Republic, as throughout Latin American, the significance of *machismo* is an integral part of the parenting and socialization of children much like *familismo*. *Machismo* includes a belief in male superiority over females, and emphasizes the development and exhibition of traditionally "masculine" characteristics such as strength, virility, and the ability to work physically hard and provide for and protect one's family. This is evident in the gender roles emphasized within families, where girls are kept close to the home and are expected to care for their families, while boys are allowed more freedom of movement because they are expected to become strong providers and protectors (Lopez, 2003). As a result of these cultural values, parents are stricter and more protective of girls and more lenient with boys, whom may not be watched as carefully as girls.

The cultural expectations and the different pressures put on boys and girls within diverse Latino families (Zambrana, 1995) could affect education and performance in school. Specifically, as girls are kept closer to home and prepared for life as a future mother, wife and caregiver, there might be a greater emphasis placed on education for girls than boys, especially if being a mother means helping the children with their schooling. For boys, it isn't that performance in school might be explicitly discouraged, but rather perhaps it is not emphasized to the same extent as it is for girls. This would be supported by the perception that education is a feminine and not masculine activity, and by the often unspoken assumption that parent involvement in education means the *mother's* involvement in education. Moreover, as boys need to learn to provide and go to work, especially since they come from low-income immigrant families for whom what constitutes "work" in Providence and in the Dominican Republic is likely physical in nature, their performance in school might be less closely watched. Thus, parents may be more lenient with boys when it comes to school, and scrutinize the grades of daughters more than those of their sons. Furthermore, because many of the children do not have a father in the home, perhaps the boys, however young they are, may be expected to fill the shoes of the "man of the house," which intentionally or not could place less of an emphasis on their schooling.

Given these cultural characteristics, both boys and girls might have a bilingual preference indicating strong cultural ties and communication within the family; however the impact on performance in school would be different. Specifically, there might be culturally-based pressure placed on girls to do well in school and less recognition of the importance of education for boys (Lopez, 2003). For girls bilingual preference might reflect the expectation both at home and in school to do well academically, whereas for boys this might not be the case. For boys, bilingual preference might reflect that they are becoming Dominican boys, which has certain expectations, and at the same time acculturating to life as Black and Latino boys in the US, which presents certain challenges and does not emphasize success in school. These dynamics would be exacerbated by the fact that the children in Providence are subject to "grossly inadequate schools" (Bailey 2002, p.20), which hinder their ability to learn.

However, what could explain the results of the longitudinal model which found that bilingual preference is negatively predictive of school performance for boys? Why might boys who prefer English do better than those who prefer bilingualism? Bailey's (2002) study of

Dominican high school students in Providence can help understand this finding. In Providence, Dominicans are profoundly affected by the racially stratified society in the US which is poignantly evident in Providence, especially socioeconomic inequalities, residential segregation, and segregated schools. Dominicans have little contact with whites and middle and upper income people. Thus, children and youth are growing up in an urban, poor/low-income, non-white environment that shapes the options afforded to them. In this context, Dominican youth in Providence think of themselves as non-white and identify with and have solidarity with their Latino and Black neighbors and peers. Thus, they share a youth culture with Black and Latino youth. If Bailey (2002) found this among Dominican adolescents, it is likely that younger Dominican children have, or are developing, the same identity, social orientation, and peer relationships.

The negative notion assigned to "acting white" has been observed among poor/low-income Black and Latino youth, especially in poor performing and segregated schools. Acting white refers to the perception that one betrays one's culture by subscribing to white cultural norms, in particular adopting the social expectations and standards of a white society, such as doing well in school. It is a self-destructive attitude, and a form of internalized oppression; it reflects internalized attitudes that perpetuate the inequalities that gave rise to the idea of white children being smart and doing well in school, whereas black and brown children are of comparably poorer intelligence and do not do well academically. Therefore, doing well in school is sometimes perceived as a sign of weakness among poor black and Latino youth, especially in cities where there is a preponderance of inadequate, segregated schools.

The notion of acting white is arguably more powerful for boys than girls, especially if girls are kept closer to the home and watched more carefully than boys who might be more influenced by things beyond the home and family. Dominican boys may be acculturating to the social standards and expectations of Black and Latino youth in the community, and the stigma associated with acting white, or doing well in school, could be manifesting itself among children in middle childhood. Acting white among Dominican children, in particular boys, may mean preferring English, which would result in them performing better in school because they have chosen to act white- speak English-

and do well in school. Furthermore, boys may be choosing to act white because they are rejecting their Black, Latino or Dominican identity and culture. Given the stigma associated with being Black or Latino, especially a Black or Latino male, that is so pervasive in the US, maybe the boys who are doing better in school are those who are rejecting their culture and language, trying to shed the stigma of being Black or brown. Boys who prefer English might do better in school that those with a bilingual preference, and those who prefer bilingualism might do worse because they do not want to act white or be white.

This was a study of acculturation, and as such it helps to understand where this particular group of children is in their acculturation. If the home and school contexts, as well as the wider society, communicate to girls that they should do well in school, this would suggest they present complementary models and expectations of academic performance. If language preference is thought of as an indicator of children's comfort moving between cultures, then, for girls, bilingual preference may lead to higher levels of achievement because the two contexts are compatible and girls are therefore comfortable moving between cultures, to their ultimate success. For boys, however, perhaps the message they are receiving about academic performance from home, school and the wider society, is not as clear and possibly conflicted. Perhaps the home and school cultures are not compatible for them, a dis-congruence that might be complicated by the larger social messages they receive. In which case, it could be that the effects of bilingual preference on academic performance shown in the longitudinal analysis indicate difficulty moving between cultures. If so, the results might say something about the cultures the boys are trying to move between, as opposed to indicating a problem at the individual level with boys having a bilingual preference.

Conclusion

It possible that school-level factors could help to explain academic performance, for all the children but in particular for the boys. Although an association between the language spoken in the school, and academic performance and child language was not identified, perhaps other school level factors could bear impact on academic achievement. Minority and immigrant children are more likely to attend segregated, low quality, overcrowded urban schools, factors that have been definitively linked to lower levels of academic performance. Additionally, perhaps social pressures and (low) expectations of Dominican boys, could explain some of the variability in academic performance. These questions were not in scope of this study and the data for this research were not appropriate for examining school-level effects, as children attended so many different schools. However, future research should explore these issues. Nevertheless, that language can explain some of the variability in academic outcomes for girls but not boys is an important finding. That such a stark difference exists along gender lines is powerful- and no other research to date has uncovered such results. Future research should seek to understand why.

There is limited understanding of cultural and familial dynamics; cultural, social and familial expectations as they pertain to education, and how such pressures and expectations might be different for boys and girls and shape children's acculturative pathways and ability to become part of the U.S. social fabric. It is imperative to increase understanding of the protective factors that help boys and girls thrive and do well in school and throughout life, at the intersection of race/ethnicity, socioeconomic status, as well as immigrant status, language and gender. Therefore, research on Dominicans, as well as other immigrant national groups, is needed. With regard to Caribbean Latinos, who are of Afro-Caribbean heritage, understanding how language and culture interact with race and gender is needed, as being black in the U.S. is a distinct experience separate from being black in other countries in the Americas; it is an experience that unfolds differently for and means different things for males and females. As the largest ethnic minority group, how diverse Latino groups fit into our socio-cultural and racial landscape is an important issue for the nation, as this impacts acculturation and adjustment, which impact education, and subsequently shape health and socioeconomic status throughout life. Immigration from Latin America is challenging the black-white racial paradigm as Latinos do not fit neatly into either box. Given the historical and deeply entrenched role of race in America, and the current anti-immigrant climate, understanding what this means for the New Americans, is crucial.

CHAPTER 8

Closing Thoughts

Increased immigration has raised many important policy issues. Some of the most vexing issues, however, relate to culture and language, as evidenced by the debate over national identity, national language, the growing number of state and local level English only laws and policies, and concerns that immigrants today are not "assimilating" (Alba & Nee, 2003; Del Valle, 2003; Peréa & García Coll, 2008). Two important points should be considered in terms of the possible policy implications of this research. First, immigration today is different from earlier waves of immigration during 1880-1920, not only because today's immigrants are coming primarily from Latin America and to a lesser degree Asia, rather than Europe; but also because technological advances allow immigrants to maintain ties to their home country, unlike earlier immigrants who were unable to do so. Immigrants today, such as the Dominican families in this study, frequently travel back and forth to visit family, communicate regularly via phone and email, and send money and goods to their families abroad. Thus, present day immigrant communities are in effect transnational populations, and immigrants and their children binational in that they often live with their feet in two countries (Alba & Nee, 2003). The second point is the importance of conceptualizing diversity in all its forms as a resource. Traditionally, studies of racial/ethnic minority groups and immigrants have operated within a cultural deficit model (García Coll & Magnuson, 1999). In stark contrast to this, this research framed bilingualism as a resource and diversity is an asset, not liabilities.

In his study of Dominicans in Providence, Bailey (2002) describes a vibrant community characterized by a mix of Dominican as well as Black and Latino urban culture. In addition to the close ties between the

Providence Dominican community and their families and communities abroad, immigrant parents are deeply rooted in their Dominican culture, and the Dominican Republic serves as their frame of reference. Their second generation children, however, exhibit the characteristics and adaptations of children living in two cultures and between two countries. Second generation youth acculturate in some ways to the culture of marginalized urban youth of color, but they do not assimilate, and maintain the language and cultural practices of the Dominican Republic that characterizes their families. For example, youth share linguistic and stylistic characteristics with their Black and Latino peers, but at home they speak Spanish with their family, eat Dominican food, and listen and dance to Caribbean music (Bailey, 2002). Thus, Dominicans in Providence are a bicultural population.

This research was about language preference and academic performance. The results for the girls are easier to interpret and indicate a need to build on bilingualism as an asset. Although the results for the boys are not as straightforward, there is insufficient evidence to conclude that bilingualism is a liability for boys, especially in light of other research. Thus, policy recommendations should be asset based, and address the importance of maintaining the Spanish language while learning English. This is supported by the work of Wong-Fillmore (1991), who presents compelling evidence for maintaining the home language while learning English. In her study of language-shift among primarily Latino language minority children in the US, Wong-Fillmore describes the detrimental effects of subtractive-bilingualism, which refers to the concept of learning a second language at the expense of losing the first. In households where parents primarily spoke a language other than English and the home language was being displaced, parents of children who were learning English but losing the home language experienced a negative change in language patterns between parents and children. Specifically, in homes where parents spoke little to no English (as is the case with the Dominican parents in this study), and where changes in family language patterns were lead by children learning English, "there was little genuine parent-child communication in such situations" (Wong-Fillmore, 1991, p.338). Wong-Fillmore concluded, "loss [of the home language] can be highly disruptive on family relations" (Wong-Fillmore, 1991, p.343). Deterioration in family communication can alienate parents from their children and cause a breakdown in parental authority and in children's respect for their parents. As the future of the nation in large part hinges on the academic success of, overwhelmingly Latino, children of immigrant families, this is an outcome that must be avoided.

These findings highlight the importance of children maintaining the home language while they learn English so as not hinder parent-child communication, which could have profound negative consequences on their performance in school. This is supported by research by Portes and Rumbaut (2001) who found that loss of the home/family language was strongly associated with cultural dissonance, namely increased parent-child conflict, which had a consistently strong, negative effect on academic achievement. They proposed that as second generation children increasingly acculturate to U.S. culture, losing the home/family language and culture, they gradually lose their drive to achieve in school, resulting in lower grades. This might be at least partially attributable to a lower level of parent involvement, poorer parent-child relationships, and children not adopting their parent's values, views and educational expectations-factors that are intimately connected to language. In light of these findings, policies should seek to support maintenance of the home language among Dominican children while learning English.

In addition to better communication, maintenance of the home language is associated with cultural transmission, and parents being able to clearly and effectively communicate values and expectations to their children. The consequences language loss poses in this regard are perhaps best stated by Wong-Fillmore (1991):

"When parents are unable to talk to their children, they cannot easily convey to them their values, beliefs, understandings, or wisdom about how to cope with their experiences. They cannot teach them about the meaning of work, or about personal responsibility, or what it means to be a moral or ethical person in a world with too many choices and too few guideposts to follow. What is lost are the bits of advice, the *consejos* parents should be able to offer children in their everyday interactions with them. Talk is a crucial link between parents and children: It is how parents impart their cultures to their children and enable them to become the kind of men and women they want them to be. When parents lose the means of socializing and influencing their children, rifts develop and families lose the intimacy that comes from shared beliefs and understandings." (p.343)

Thus, policies should seek to build cultural capital as a resource, encouraging maintenance of the home language and culture among new immigrants while learning English. This will foster communication and understanding between parents and children, and support parents in the parenting, socialization, and enculturation of their children.

Policy Significance

Increased immigration has raised many important questions and policy issues regarding the integration of immigrants. As the U.S. historical record shows, it is during periods of high immigration like today, when anti-immigrant sentiments are high, that issues of language come to the fore and so-called foreign languages and the people who speak them are perceived by many as a threat to the nation (Peréa & García Coll, 2008). Today, these sentiments are clearly directed at Latinos and the Spanish language. Perhaps Harvard University Professor Samuel Huntington best sums up the "threat hypothesis" in his essay The Hispanic Challenge (2004):

"The persistent inflow of Hispanic immigrants threatens to divide the United States into two peoples, two cultures and two languages. Unlike past immigrant groups, Mexicans and other Latinos have not assimilated into mainstream US culture, forming instead their own political and linguistic enclaves... and rejecting the Anglo-Protestant values that built the American dream. The United States ignores this challenge at its peril (¶ 1)."

The controversy over language is perhaps most evident and contentious in education. In the last ten years, the federal Bilingual Education Act has been allowed to expire and bilingual education programs across the country have been dismantled through voter referenda- even though the number of children who speak a language other than English has increased and continues to grow. Today, the use of languages other than English, especially Spanish, is not advocated or supported within our institutions, is often explicitly discouraged, and lacks much popular or political support. Consequently, during the last thirty years there has been a clear shift in language education policy in schools. This shift has been from bilingual education programs that, in varying degrees, support maintenance of the home/family language, to widespread implementation of English immersion and early-exit transitional bilingual education programs. These programs do not promote maintenance of the home/family language and instead emphasize English language acquisition in the least amount of time possible. The primary goal is for children in these programs to transition from using the home/family language to the English language in school- even though this has profound implications for linguistic and cultural dynamics within the home, which are intimately tied to parent-child relationships and thus academic performance (Portes & Rumbaut, 2001; Rumbaut, 1995, 1999; Suarez-Orozco & Suarez-Orozco, 1995, 2001).

Bilingualism or use of a language other than English has traditionally been thought of as a liability, thus the likelihood that preservation of a language other than English might be an asset for immigrant and language minority children, and that greater English usage and English monolingualism might pose certain risks, is highly controversial. Nevertheless, although the research findings are somewhat mixed, as was the case in this study, the research overall indicates that maintenance of non-English languages while acquiring English is associated with higher levels of academic performance among children of immigrant families. Thus, bilingualism/biculturalism appears to be a better acculturation path for immigrants. This confirms theoretical positions of acculturation and lends credence to the need to encourage and support maintenance of the home/family language among immigrants *while learning English,* as it is associated with academic performance and thus has particular implications for schools. Given that education is the strongest predictor of long term health and socio-economic status, the implications of this provocative finding are profound and arguably call for a paradigm shift.

However, legitimate questions about language use among immigrants remain, especially given that English language proficiency is a basic necessity in today's increasingly competitive, English dominated globalized world. But in the US, English has always been essential for upward for upward mobility, something immigrants to this country have always known. After all, perhaps no one knows the power and value of English more than an immigrant who doesn't speak English. Unfortunately, these legitimate and important questions often come tandem with concerns- fears- about threats to our national identity, and the ability, and willingness, of immigrants to integrate into the mainstream US social fabric; concerns and fears which, in this case, are not supported by the extant research. Current evidence indicates that linguistic assimilation among immigrants today is occurring at a faster rate than ever before (Peréa & García Coll, 2008). Across generations, there is a switch to English monolingualism that is completed by the third generation, if not before. This is evident in areas of the US, such as Los Angeles and Miami, which have a consistent and steady flow of Spanish speaking im/migrants, and are saturated with Spanish speakers populating well established Spanish speaking Latino communities. As stated by Professor Rubén Rumbaut in recent Congressional testimony: "the power of assimilative forces is nowhere clearer than in the linguistic switch across the generations" (Comprehensive Immigration Reform, 2007).

Although the US is a diverse, multilingual country, which in large part has been historically shaped by immigration, Americans are not known for their language skills. This is perhaps best captured by the following joke:

What do you call someone who speaks many languages?
Multilingual

What about someone who speaks two languages?
Bilingual

What do you call someone who speaks only one language?
American

This highlights how the US has historically been a country that has absorbed millions of immigrants from all over the world, but not their languages, a "language graveyard," if you will (Comprehensive Immigration Reform, 2007 p.22). This is the case for Spanish speakers today. Although some might interpret this trend as a good thing for the nation, the consequences might not be so good. Knowing what maintaining the home/family language means for relationships between immigrant children and their parents (Portes and Rumbaut, 2001; Wong-Fillmore, 1991), what it likely means for children's ability to achieve in school and beyond, as discussed throughout this text, and the consequences for those same children if the language is lost, do not bode well for the future of this country, a future which is contingent upon the success and positive integration of immigrants and their children. English is not in any danger, however, as stated by Professor Rumbaut, "what is endangered... is the survivability of the non-English languages that immigrants bring with them to the United States" (Comprehensive Immigration Reform, 2007, p.22). As argued throughout this text, language is an asset, not a liability, and maintaining, encouraging, and fostering this asset among those who possess it, is desirable.

Nevertheless, English language learner students, who are overwhelmingly Spanish speaking Latino children, increasingly find themselves in schools that do not promote preservation of the home/family language while learning English. Given that maintenance of the home language seems appears to be a resource that functions as a protective factor for immigrant children, although there is variability and the mechanisms by which this operates require further study, what is needed are school policies that promote English language acquisition while maintaining the native language, or at least present parents and their children with a genuine choice for them to make an informed decision about the education of their children which they feel is in their child's and family's best interest. In other words, what are needed are policies that endorse and foster bilingualism. However, such policies should not be restricted to immigrant populations as there are clear benefits to bilingualism for all people and the need for fluency in a language other than English reflects the demands of our changing times. Peréa and García Coll (2008) help to illustrate this point:

> "Just as there is a need to learn English, there are clear reasons
> to learn a second language and become bilingual. In an era of
> globalization and increased immigration, the value of
> multilingualism goes without explanation. The ability to

effectively communicate cannot be overstated, and the more languages a person speaks the more people a person is able to communicate with. The job market advantages of being able to communicate in more than one language are clear. For these reasons, it would seem in the best interest of the nation to build on the strengths and abilities of its new immigrants and for the government to adopt policies that promote bilingualism as an asset (pp. 217-218)."

This study has strong implications for language policy as well as the broader policy arena. Other factors impact academic performance; certainly language is not the only one. It has been definitively established that race and socioeconomic status have profound implications for education, and this is particularly true for minority students. This research indicates that the predictive power of language differs along gender lines, distinctions that perhaps, at least in part, reflect matters of race/ethnicity, and likely socio-economic status, and how they interact with sex and acculturation. This indicates that the competencies of children vary within ethnic groups (for example girls differ from boys), probably resulting from the interaction of cultural and social factors. This suggests that the challenges people face, the factors that put people at risk, and the protective elements that can mitigate the effects of those factors, differ as well, reflecting the basic tenets of ecological theory and the idea of development in context.

For policy to be effective what is needed is not a one-size-fits all policy approach, but rather a group of policies that are sensitive to the unique needs and circumstances of distinct groups. Thus, policies must be flexible and adaptable so the programs and services policies define are (culturally) appropriate and most effective in their delivery and application. This is appropriate given the profound demographic shifts underway. The U.S. population is changing, driven in large part by immigration from Latin America. The new immigrants today do not fit neatly into any one demographic box and have needs and concerns that cross those of diverse racial/ethnic and cultural groups.

The importance of cultural competence in the delivery of programs and services is well understood and supported by the research literature, and policy should reflect the same level of understanding. The existence of a policy implies the recognition of a social need and some level of governmental responsibility for addressing it. Thus, an efficient and effective policy approach would be one that takes a broad approach to addressing social issues. As policy by definition is a deliberate plan of action to guide decisions and achieve (rational) outcomes, and as social policies aim to meet human needs and improve human welfare, policy should be based on an ecological model that understands the many contexts and environmental factors that impact people's lives and life chances. As the developmental trajectories and competencies of people vary across and within groups, so does it logically follow that the path from point A to point B likely varies as well. As policies define the opportunities that define those paths, they should be able to accommodate similarities and differences. In order to achieve this, broad federal policies, such as No Child Left Behind, as well as state-level policies, such as language education policies, should be matched with more specific municipal and community level policies and programs that can more accurately speak to the needs and concerns of their particular communities.

Conclusions

Early immigrants became an integral part of the U.S. social fabric and played a key role in shaping this country's landscape, as did Native Americans, African peoples, and northern European immigrants who arrived in the US before the mass waves of immigration at the turn of the twentieth century. It is difficult to imagine this country without pizza and beer, creole cooking, California wine, Chinese or Indian food, let alone the distinctly regional characteristics of New England, the southwest, or the diversity of our large urban areas such as New York, Miami, and Los Angeles, places and regions that are characterized by the many diverse people and cultures who came together there, called it home, and created these distinctly "American" places. Earlier immigrants found ways to integrate into U.S. society, and today's immigrants will find ways to integrate as well- but they must be supported and given appropriate paths if they are to achieve that. New immigrants today are different from previous immigrants. Not only are they primarily from within the hemisphere, but they move back and forth and maintain close ties with their home country; they do not sever familial, cultural or linguistic connections as in the past. Policies should respond to the cultural characteristics and dynamics of immigration today and endeavor to sustain and develop the cultural resources immigrants possess as assets for the nation.

Globalization is putting pressure on our institutions, and requiring that we adapt as individuals and as a nation in order to successfully participate and compete in an ever more demanding and competitive world. People are moving, borders are arguably becoming (more) fluid, and the cultural and linguistic characteristics of nation states are changing as a result of population shifts driven by changes in birth rates and global migration. In our increasingly interconnected world where commerce, communication, and the movement of people and ideas are no longer restricted or defined by cultural and sociopolitical borders, the need to be able to transcend and negotiate borders and build on differences, is paramount. Our new and ever changing world requires people to have the skills to work, collaborate and cooperate across borders, cultures and languages. As such our unique cultural resources should be nurtured and developed, not squandered.

Notes

Chapter 1: Introduction
1. The US Census Bureau defines linguistically isolated households as households where no person over the age of fourteen speaks only English, or households where no person over the age of fourteen, who speaks a language other than English, speaks English at least very well.

Chapter 3: Literature Review
1. The first generation refers to foreign-born children who immigrated to the U.S. with their parents, and the second-generation refers to children born in the U.S. to immigrant parents.
2. The test is administered in English first followed by an opportunity for test-takers to respond to questions in her/his native language.
3. Children were interviewed up to five times over the three years of the study and were asked about their ethnic/racial identities; perception of ethnic/racial group status and racial/ethnic discrimination; attitudes towards school; educational expectations and aspirations; perceptions of teachers; language comfort; peer relationships; and in/out group comfort. Parents were interviewed in the second year of data collection and were asked about their families immigration history; demographic background; education and work; household composition; family, ethnic, and cultural values and beliefs; ethnic/cultural practices; language comfort; income and assets; and beliefs and practices regarding their child's education. Each child's teacher completed two questionnaires for each child in the study, one on her/his

thoughts on individual children and impressions of each child as compared to other children in her/his class; and the other regarding pedagogy and questions about what helped children do better in school. In addition, with parental consent, school academic records containing grades, test scores, absenteeism and lateness were obtained from the schools for each child in the study. School administrative records were also obtained and provide data on school poverty levels and ethnic/racial composition for each child's school. Lastly, a detailed ethnography of each immigrant community was conducted in the first year, and a social history was completed in the third year. These help to contextualize the experiences of these children and the immigration experiences of their families.

4. In Transitional Bilingual Education programs English Language Learner students have some degree of instruction in the native/first language (L1) for a determined period of time. The goal is transition to English-only instruction as quickly as possible. In Maintenance Bilingual Education programs, English Language Learner students receive instruction in both the native/first language (L1), and English or the second language (L2). The goal is academic and language proficiency in both languages.

Appendix A

Measures

Child language preference

Five questions:

1. *Which language do you like to speak more, English or [Spanish]? Or do you like them both the same?*
2. *Do you like to have people speak to you in English or [Spanish]? Or do you like them both the same?*
3. *Do you like to watch TV and movies in [Spanish] or in English? Or do you like them both the same?*
4. *Would you like to have your teachers teach in English or [Spanish]? Or do you like them both the same?*
5. *When people read or tell you stories, what do you like more: to hear stories in English or in [Spanish]? Or do you like them both the same?*

Mother's language use

Two questions that had scaled answer choices. The response options were (1) only Spanish, (2) more Spanish than English, (3) both Spanish and English equally, (4) more English than Spanish, (5). The questions were:

1. *What languages do you speak?*
2. *What language(s) do you speak to [child]?*

Mother's language comfort.

Four questions. The parent answered yes or no to the question. If they answered yes, they were asked *How comfortable are you doing this?* The scaled answer choices were (1) uncomfortable, (2) comfortable, and (3) very comfortable. The questions were:

1. *Do you communicate in English with neighbors who were born in the US?*
2. *Do you talk to people at work in English?*

3.   *Do you talk to strangers on the phone in English?*
4.   *Do you speak English with people at your child's school?*

Language spoken in the school

Data on each child's educational program type obtained from school records. The program types were regular education, bilingual education/ESL, and bilingual/special education.

Teacher's feelings on family language use

Each child's teacher completed a fifteen item questionnaire on her/his educational practice with responses on a nine point scale ranging from 1=strongly agree, 5=in between, and 9=strongly disagree. The questionnaire was not specific to each child. One statement to which teachers were asked to respond dealt with the effect of English language usage in the home. The question was:

"Children do better in school if they come from families where English is regularly spoken."

This measure is the response to that question.

School composition

The number/percent of Latino and language minority children, obtained from school administrative records.

School engagement

Eight questions that had scaled answer choices. The response options were (1) not at all important, (2) not as important, (3) in between, (4) pretty important, (5) very important. The questions were:

1.   *How important is it to you that you get good grades?*

2.   *How important is it to you that you stay out of trouble at school?*

3.   *How important is it to you that your teacher like you?*

4.   *How important is it to you that you do your homework?*

5.   *How important is it to you that you go to school every day?*

6.   *How important is it to you that you graduate from high school?*

7.   *How important is it to you that you have friends in school?*

8.   *How important is it to you that you try hard in school?*

Parent involvement in education
Parent's response to the scaled question "On a scale of 1-7, with 7 being very involved, how involved should parents be in their child's education?"

Mother's level of education in years
Response to the question, *"How many years of school have you had?"*

Annual income
Response to the scaled question, *"What is your annual household income right now?"* The response options were (1) $0-$4,999, (2) $5,000-$9,999, (3) $10,000-$14,999, (4) $15,000-$19,999, (5) $20,000-$29,999, (6) $30,000-$39,999 (7) $40,000-$49,999, (8) $50,000-$59,999, (9) $60,000 and over

The number of places the family has lived in since the child started school
Response to the question, *"How many places have you lived in since (child) began school?*

Single parent
Binary 0=no, 1=yes

Sex
Binary 0=male, 1=female

Cohort (age cohort)
Binary 0= younger cohort, 1=older cohort

References

Alba, R., & Nee, V. (2003). *Remaking the American mainstream: assimilation and contemporary immigration.* Cambridge, MA: Harvard University Press.

Alexander, K. L., Entwisle, D. R., & Kabbani, N. S. (2001). The dropout process in life course perspective: Early risk factors at home and school. *Teachers College Record, 103,* 760-822.

Alexander, K., Entwistle, D. R. & Horsey, C. S. (1997). From first grade forward: early foundations of high school dropouts. *Sociology of education,* 70 (2), 87-107.

Aud, S., Hussar, W., Planty, M., Snyder, T., Bianco, K., Fox, M., Frohlich, L., Kemp, J., & Drake, L. (2010). *The condition of education 2010* (NCES 2010-028). Washington, DC: National Center for Education Statistics, Institute of Education Sciences, U.S. Department of Education. Retrieved from: http://nces.ed.gov/ pubs2010/2010028.pd f.

Bailey, B. (2002) *Language, race, and negotiation of identity: A study of Dominican Americans.* New York, NY: LFB Scholarly Publishing LLC.

Bailey, B. (2000). *The Providence Dominican community: Some aspects of immigration and ethnicity.* Unpublished manuscript.

Baker, K. A., & de Kanter, A. A. (1983). An answer from research on bilingual education. *American Education, 56 (4),* 157-169.

Berry, J. W., Poortinga, Y. H., Segall, M. H., & Dasen, P. R. (1992). *Cross Cultural Psychology: Research and applications.* Cambridge, UK: Cambridge University Press.

Brandon, P. 1991. Gender differences in young Asian Americans' educational attainment. Sex Roles, 25: 45-61.

Bronfenbrenner, U. (1979). *The ecology of human development: experiments by nature and design.* Cambridge, MA: Harvard University Press.

Brown, E. R., Wyn, R., Yu, H., Valenzuela, A., & Dong, L. (1999). Access to Health Insurance and Health Care for Children in Immigrant Families. In Hernandez, D. J. (Ed.), *Children of immigrants: Health, adjustment, and public assistance* (pp. 125-186). Washington, DC: National Academy Press.

Capps, R., Fix, M., Ost, J., Reardon-Anderson, J., Passel, J. S. (2005). *The health and well being of young children of immigrants.* Washington, DC: The Urban Institute. Retrieved from http://urban.org/Uploaded PDF/311139_ChildrenImmigrants.pdf

Clark, K. B., & Clark, M. K. (1974). Racial identification and preference in Negro children. In T. M. Newcomb & E. L. Hartley (Eds.), *Readings in social psychology.* New York, NY: Holt.

Clark, K. B., & Clark, M. K. (1940). Skin color as a factor in racial identification of negro preschool children. *Journal of Social Psychology, S.P.S.S.I. Bulletin,* 11, 159-169.

Clark, K. B., & Clark, M. K. (1939). The development of consciousness of self and emergence of racial identification in negro preschool children. *Journal of Social Psychology, S.P.S.S.I. Bulletin,* 10, 591-599

Comprehensive Immigration Reform: Becoming Americans- US Immigrant Integration. Hearing before the subcommittee on immigration, citizenship, refugees, border security, and international law (Serial 110-27), 110 Cong 21 (2007) (testimony of Rubén Rumbaut).

Cosentino de Cohen, C., Deterding, N., & Clewell, B.C. (2005). *Whose left behind?: Immigrant children in high and low lep schools.* Washington, DC: The Urban Institute. Retrieved from: http://urban.org/UploadedPDF/411231_whos_left_behind.pdf

Crawford, J. (2000). *At war with diversity: US language policy in an age of anxiety.* Clevedon, England: Multilingual Matters, Ltd.

Cummins, J. (1991). Language development and academic learning. In L. M. Malavé & G. Duquette (Eds.), *Language, culture, and cognition* (pp. 161-175). Clevedon, England: Multilingual Matters.

Cummins, J. (1992). Bilingual education and English immersion: The Ramirez report in theoretical perspective. *Bilingual Research Journal, 16 (1&2),* 91-104.

Davis, J. W. & Bauman, K. J. (2008). *School enrollment in the United States: 2006,* current population reports, P20-559. Washington, DC: U.S. Census Bureau. Retrieved from: http://www.census.gov/prod/2008 pubs/p20-559.pdf).

Delgado-Gaitán, C. (1992). School matters in the Mexican-American home: Socializing children to education. *American Educational Research Journal, 29 (3),* 495-513.

Del Valle, S. (2003). *Language rights and the law in the United States: Finding our voices.* Clevedon, England: Multilingual Matters.

Duncan, G., & Brooks-Gunn, J.(2000). Family Poverty, Welfare Reform and Child Development. *Child Development, 71*(1), 188-196.

Eccles, J. S., Midgley, C., & Adler, T. (1984). Grade-related changes in the school environment; Effects on academic achievement motivation. In J. G. Nicholls (Ed.), *Advances in motivation and achievement, Vol 3* (pp. 283-331). Greenwhich, CT: IAI.

Falcon, L. M., Tucker, K. L. & Bermudez, O. (1997) *Correlates of Poverty and Participation in Food Assistance Programs among Hispanic Elders in Massachusetts.* Institute for Research on Poverty, Discussion Paper no. 1121-97.

Feliciano, C. (2001). The benefits of biculturalism: Exposure to immigrant culture and dropping out of school among Asian and Latino youths. *Social Science Quarterly,* 82(4), 865-879.

Feliciano, C. (2006). Unequal origins: Immigrant selection and the education of the second generation. New York: LFB Scholarly Publishing, LLC.

Feliciano, C., & Rumbaut, R. G. (2005). Gendered paths: Educational and occupational expectations and outcomes among adult children of immigrants. *Ethnic and racial studies, Vol 28 (6) (November),* 1087-1118.

Fernandez, R. M.,& Nielsen, F. (1986). Bilingualism and Hispanic scholastic achievement: some baseline results. *Social Science Research,* 14, 43–70.

Fillmore, L. W. (1991). When learning a second language means losing the first. *Early Childhood Research Quarterly, 6,* 323-346.

Finn, J. D., & Rock, D. A. (1997). Academic success among students at risk for school failure. *Journal of Applied Psychology, 82,* 221-234.

Fix, M., & Passel, J. S. (2003). *U.S. immigration: trends and implications for schools.* Paper presented at the National Association for Bilingual Education, NCLB Implementation Institute, New Orleans, LA, January 28-29. Retrieved from: http://www.urban.org/url.cfm?ID=410654.

Fuligni, A. (1997). The academic achievement of adolescents from immigrant families: the roles of family background, attitudes, and behavior. *Child Development, 68,* 351-363.

LaFromboise, T., Coleman, H. L., & Gerton, J. (1993). Psychological impact of biculturalism: Evidence and theory. Psychological Bulletin, 114 (3), 395-412.

Funkhouser, E. & Ramos, F. (1993). The choices of migration destination: Dominican and Cuban immigrants to the mainland United States and Puerto Rico. *International Migration Review, 27 (3)*: 537-556.

García Coll, C., Akiba, D., Palacios, N., Bailey, B., Silver, R., DiMartino, L., & Chin, C. (2002). Parental involvement in children's education: lessons from three immigrant groups. *Parenting: Science and Practice, 2 (3),* 303-324.

García Coll, C., & Magnuson, K. (1999). Theory and research with children of color: implications for social policy. In H. E. Fitzgerald, B. M. Lester, & B. S. Zuckerman (Eds.), *Children of color: research health and policy issues* (pp.219-255). New York, NY: Garland Publishing, Inc.

García Coll, C., & Marks, A. K. (2009). *Immigrant stories: Identity and academic pathways during middle childhood.* New York, NY: Oxford University Press.

García Coll, C., Szalacha, L. A., & Palacios, N. (2005). Children of Dominican, Portuguese, and Cambodian immigrant families: Academic attitudes and pathways during middle childhood. In R. C. Cooper, C. T. Garcia Coll, W. T. Bartko, H. Davis, & C. Chatman (Eds.), *Developmental pathways through middle childhood: Rethinking contexts and diversity as resources* (pp. 207-233). Mahwah, NJ: Lawrence Erlbaum Associates.

Gefen, D., Straub D. W., Boudreau, M. C. (2000) Structural equation modeling and regression: guidelines for research practice, Communications of the Association for Information Systems, 4 (7), 1-70.

Gonzalez, J. (2001). *Harvest of empire: A history of Latinos in America.* New York, NY: Penguin Books.

Greene, J.P. (1997). A meta-analysis of the Rossell and Baker review of bilingual education research. *Bilingual Research Journal, 21 (2&3)*. Retrieved from: http://brj.asu.edu/articlesv2/green.html

Grieco, E. M. (2009). *Race and Hispanic origin of the foreign-born population in the United States: 2007,* American community survey reports, ACS-11. Washington, DC: U.S. Census Bureau. Retrieved from: http://www.census.gov/prod/2010pubs/acs-11.pdf.

Gringlas, M. & Weinraub, M. (1995). The more things change ... Single-parenting revisited. *Journal of Family Issues, 16*, 29-52.

Hakuta, K. (1986). *Mirror of language.* New York, NY: Basic Books, Inc.

Hernandez, D. J. (2004). Demographic change and the life circumstances of immigrant families. *Future of Children, 14* (2), 17-47

Hernandez, D. J., & Darke, K. (1999). Socioeconomic and demographic risk factors and resources among children in immigrant families. In D. J. Hernandez (Ed.), *Children of immigrants* (pp. 19-126). Washington D.C.: National Academy Press.

Huntington, S. P. (2004). The Hispanic challenge. Foreign Policy (no page numbers), March/April 2004. Retrieved March 14, 2004, from http:// www.foreignpolicy.com

Huston, A. C., & Ripke, M. N. (2006). Middle childhood: Contexts of development. In A. C. Huston & M. N. Ripke (Eds), *Developmental contexts in middle childhood: Bridges to adolescence and adulthood* (pp. 1-22). New York, NY: Cambridge University Press.

Kao, G. (1999). Psychological well-being and educational achievement among immigrant youth. In, D. J. Hernandez (Ed.), *Children of Immigrants: Health, Adjustment, and Public Assistance* (pp. 410-477). Washington, DC: National Academy Press. Retrieved February 6, 2007 from: http://books.nap.edu/openbook.php?record_id=9592&page=410

Kao, G., & Tienda, M. (1995). Optimism and achievement: the educational performance of immigrant youth. *Social Science Quarterly, 76,* 1-19.

Kasinitz, P., Mollenkopf, J. H., Waters, M. C., Holdaway, J. (2008). *Inheriting the city: the children of immigrants come of age.* New York, NY: Russell Sage Foundation.

Kewal Ramani, A., Gilbertson, L., Fox, M., & Provasnik, S. (2007). *Status and trends in the education of racial and ethnic minorities* (NCES 2007-039). Washington, DC: National Center for Education Statistics, Institute of Education Sciences, U.S. Department of Education. Retrieved from: http://nces.ed.gov/pubs2007/2007039.pdf.

Larsen, L. J. (2004). *The foreign-born population in the United States: 2003.* Current population reports, P20-551. Washington, DC: U.S. Census Bureau. Retrieved from: http://www.census.gov/prod/2004pubs/p20-551.pdf.

Lee, S. (2001). More than "model minorities" or "delinquents": A look at Hmong American high school students. Harvard educational review, 71: 505-528.

Lopez, E. M., Ehly, S., & Garcia-Vasquez, E. (2002). Acculturation, social support and academic achievement of Mexican and Mexican American high schools students: An exploratory study. *Psychology in Schools*, 39(3), 245-257.

Lopez, N. (2003). *Hopeful girls, troubled boys: Race and gender disparity in urban education.* New York, NY: Routledge.

Lugalia, T., & Overturf, J. (2004). *Children and the households they live in: 2000. Census 2000 Special Reports.* Washington, DC: US Census Bureau. Retrieved from: http://www.census.gov/prod/2004pubs/censr -14.pdf

Ma, J. (2002). *What works for the children? What we know and don't know about bilingual education.* Cambridge, MA: Harvard University, the Civil Rights Project. Retrieved from: http://www.civilrightsproject.ucla.edu/research/bilingual02/bilingual_paper02.pdf

MacCallum, R. C., & Austin, J. T. (2000). Applications of structural equation modeling in psychological research. *Annual Review of Psychology,* 51, 201-226.

Marcuss, M. and R. Borgos. (2004) *Who are New England's Immigrants.* Boston, MA: Federal Reserve Bank of Boston. Retrieved from: http://www.bos.frb.org/commdev/c&b/2004/fall/Immigrants.pdf.

McLanahan, S., & Sandefur, G. (1994). *Growing up with a single parent: What hurts, what helps.* Cambridge, MA: Harvard University Press.

McLoyd, V. C. (1998). Socioeconomic disadvantage and child development. *American Psychologist, 53*, 185-204.

Migration Policy Institute (2004). *The Dominican population in the United States: Growth and distribution.* New York, NY: Migration Policy Institute. Retrieved from: http://www.migrationpolicy.org/pubs/MPI_Report_Dominican_Pop US.pdf.

National Research Council and Institute of Medicine. (2000). *From Neurons to Neighborhoods: The Science of Early Childhood Development.* Committee on Integrating the Science of Early Childhood Development. J Shonkoff & D. Phillips (Eds.). Board on Children, Youth, and Families, Commission on Behavioral and Social Sciences and Education. Washington, DC: National Academy Press.

National Research Council and Institute of Medicine. (1997). *Improving schooling for language-minority children: a research agenda.* Committee on Developing a Research Agenda on the Education of Limited-English-Proficient and Bilingual students. D. August & K. Hakuta (Eds.). Board on Children, Youth, and Families, Commission on Behavioral and Social Sciences and Education. Washington, DC: National Academy Press.

Nord, C. W., & Griffin, J. A. (1999). Educational profile of 3- to 8-year old children of immigrants. In D. J. Hernandez (Ed.), *Children of immigrants*. Washington, DC: National Academy Press.

O'Brien, R. M. (1979). The use of Pearson's r with ordinal data. *American Sociological Review, 44*, 851-857.

Okagaki, L., (2001). Parental beliefs, parenting style and children's intellectual development. In E. L. Grigorenko & R. J. Sternberg (Eds.), *Family environment and intellectual functioning: A life-span perspective* (pp. 141-172). Hillsdale, NJ: Erlbaum Associates

Peal, E., & Lambert, W. (1962). The relation of bilingualism to intelligence. *Psychological Monographs, 76*, 1-23.

Peréa, F. C., & García Coll, C. (2008). The social and cultural contexts of bilingualism. In J. Altarriba, & R. R. Heredia (Eds.), *An Introduction to Bilingualism: Principles and Processes* (pp.199-241). Mahwah, NJ: Lawrence Erlbaun Associates.

Peréa, F. C., Marks, A. K., Soursourian, M., Gerace, L., & García Coll, C. (2006). *Early academic pathways as a predictor of academic outcomes in adolescence: A longitudinal study of children of immigrants*. Presented at the Society for Research in Child Development Biennial Meeting, Boston, MA.

Pew Hispanic Center. (2009). *Hispanics of Dominican origin in the United States, 2007*. Washington, DC: Pew Research Center. Retrieved from: http://pewhispanic.org/files/factsheets/52.pdf.

Phelan P., Davidson, A. L. & Yu, H. C. (1991) Students' multiple worlds: Negotiating the boundaries of family, peer and school cultures. *Anthropology and Education Quarterly, 22*(3), 224-250.

Phelan, P. Davidson, A. L., & Yu, H. C. (1998). *Adolescent's Worlds, Negotiating Family, Peers, and Schools*. New York, NY: Teachers College Press.

Phinney, J. S., & Landin, J. (1998). Research Paradigms for studying ethnic minority families within and across groups. In, V. C. McLoyd & L. Steinberg (Eds.), *Studying minority adolescents* (pp. 89-109). Mahwah, NJ: Lawrence Earlbaum Associates, Inc.

Pong, S.-l., & Hao, L. (2007). Neighborhood and school factors in the school performance of immigrants' children. *International Migration Review,* 41(1), 206-241.

Portes, A., & Hao, L. (2004). The schooling of children of immigrants: Contextual effects on the educational attainment of the second generation. *Proceedings of the National Academy of Sciences of the United States of America, 101(33),* 11920-11927.

Portes, A., & MacLeod, D. (1999). Educating the second generation: Determinants of academic achievement among children of immigrants in the United States. *Journal of Ethnic & Migration Studies, 25*(3), 373-396.

Portes, A., & Rumbaut. R. G. (2006). *Immigrant America: A portrait (3ʳᵈ edition).* Berkeley, CA: University of California Press.

Portes, A., & Rumbaut. R. G. (2001). *Legacies: The story of the immigrant second generation.* Berkeley, CA: University of California Press.

Portes, A. & Zhou, M. (1993). The new second generation: Segmented assimilation and its variants among post-1965 immigrant youth. *The Annals of the American Academy of Political and Social Sciences,* 530, 74-96.

Rodriguez, C. M. (2001). Accommodating linguistic differences: towards a comprehensive theory of language rights in the US. *Harvard Civil Rights-Civil Liberties Law Review,* 36, 133-223.

Rong, X. L., & Brown, F. 2001.The effects of immigrant generation and ethnicity on educational attainment among young Caribbean blacks in the United States. Harvard educational review, 71: 536-565.

Rossell, C.H. & Baker, K. (1996). The effectiveness of bilingual education. *Research in the Teaching of English, 30,* 7-74.

Ruiz-de-Velasco, J., & Fix, M. (2000). Overlooked and underserved: Immigrant students in US secondary schools. Washington, DC: The Urban Institute.

Rumbaut. R. G. (1995). The new Californians: Comparative research findings on the educational progress of immigrant children. In R. G. Rumbaut & W. A. Cornelius (Eds), *California's immigrant children: Theory, research, and implications for educational policy* (pp. 17-70). La Jolla, CA: University of California, San Diego, Center for US-Mexican Studies.

Rumbaut, R. G. (1999). Assimilation and its discontents: Ironies and paradoxes. In J. DeWind, C. Hirschman, & P. Kasinitz (Eds), *The handbook of international migration: The American experience* (pp. 172-195). New York, NY: Russell Sage Foundation.

Rumbaut, R. G. (2008). The coming of the second generation: Immigration and ethnic mobility in southern California. *The ANNALS of the American academy of political and social science, Vol 620 (1),* 196-236

Rumbaut. R. G., & Portes, A. (Eds.). (2001). *Ethnicities: Children of immigrants in America.* Berkeley, CA: University of California Press.

Rumberger, R. W., & Larson, K. A. (1998). Toward explaining differences in educational achievement among Mexican American language minority students. *Sociology of Education,* 71, 68–92.

Schneider, B., Martinez, S., & Owens, A. (2006). Barriers to educational opportunities for Hispanics in the United States. In National Research Council, Panel on Hispanics in the United States, M. Tienda & F. Mitchell (Eds.), *Hispanics and the future of America (pp.179-227).* Washington, DC: National Academies Press.

Shields, M. K., & Behrman, R. E. (2004). Children of immigrant families: Analysis and recommendations. *Future of Children, 14 (2),* 4-16.

Shin, H. B. (2005). *School enrollment- social and economic characteristics of students: October 2003,* current population reports, P20-554. Washington, DC: U.S. Census Bureau. Retrieved from: http://www. census.gov/prod/2005pubs/p20-554.pdf.

Stanton-Salazar, R. D., & Dornbusch, S. M. (1995). Social capital and the reproduction of inequality: information networks among Mexican-Origin high school students." *Sociology of Education,* 68, 116–135.

Steele, C. M. (1997). A threat in the air: how stereotype shapes intelectual identity and performance. *American Psychologist,* 52 (6), 613-629.

Steele, C. M., & Aronson, J. (1995). Stereotype threat and the intelectual test performance of African Americans. *Journal of Personality and Social Psychology,* 69 (5), 797-811.

Stritikus, T. (2002). *Immigrant children and the politics of English-Only: Views from the classroom. New Americans Series.* New York, NY: LFB Scholarly Publishing.

Stritikus, T., & Manyak, P. (2000). Creating opportunities for the academic success of linguistically diverse students: What does the research say? In T. Bergeson (Ed.) *Educating limited English proficient students in Washington State.* Olympia, WA: Office of Superintendent of Public Instruction.

Suarez-Orozco, C. (2010). *In the best interest of our children: Examining our immigration enforcement policy.* Written statement prepared on behalf of the American Psychological Association, for an ad-hoc hearing of the US House of Representatives, July 15, 2010. Retrieved from: http://www.apa.org/about/gr/issues/cyf/immigration-enforceme nt.aspx

Suarez-Orozco, C., & Baolian Qin. 2002. Immigrant boys' experiences in U.S. Schools. In, M. Suarez-Orozco, C. Suarez-Orozco, & D. Baolian Qin (Eds), The new immigration: An interdisciplinary reader (pp.345-357). New York, NY: Routledge.

Suarez-Orozco, C. & Suarez-Orozco, M.. (2001). *Children of immigration.* Cambridge, MA: Harvard University Press.

Suarez-Orozco, C. & Suarez-Orozco, M. (1995). *Transformations: Immigration, family life, and achievement motivation among Latino adolescents.* Stanford, CA: Stanford University Press.

Thomas, W. P., & Collier, V. (1997). *School effectiveness for language minority students.* Washington, DC: National Clearinghouse for Bilingual Education. Retrieved from www.ncela.gwu.edu/ncbepubs/ resource/effectiveness/Thomas-collier97.pdf

Thomas, W. P., & Collier, V. (2001). *A national study of school effectiveness for language minority students' long-term academic achievement.* Center for Research on Education, Diversity and Excellence. Retrieved from: http://www.crede.ucsc.edu/research/llaa/1.1_final. html

Valdés, G. (1996). *Con respeto: Bridging the distance between culturally diverse families and schools, an ethnographic portrait.* New York, NY: Teacher College Press.

Waters, M. 1996. The intersection of gender, race and ethnicity in identity development in Caribbean American teens. In B. J. R. Leadbeater & N. Way (Eds.), Urban girls: resisting stereotypes, creating identities (pp. 65-84). New York, NY: New York University Press.

Willig, A.C. (1985). A meta-analysis of selected studies on the effectiveness of bilingual education. *Review of Educational Research, 55(3),* 269-317.

Zambrana, R. E. (Ed.) (1995). *Understanding Latino families: Scholarship, policy, and practice.* Sage Publications. Newbury Park, CA: Sage Publications.

Index

Academic achievement, 27, 44, 45, 54, 56, 77, 109, 110, 111, 125, 128, 135, 136, 155
  Gender, 56, 58, 60, 62, 112, 129, 130, 136, 139, 140, 141, 143, 144
  Generation, 35
  Immigrant status, 28, 35, 37, 38, 64, 151
  Race, 35, 39, 56
  vs. US natives, 53, 54, 55, 151
Acting white, 149
Alba & Nee, 153
Assimilation, vii, 9, 10, 29, 37, 38, 42, 44, 62, 63, 70, 73, 74, 78, 159
August, 55
Bailey, 12, 14, 15, 18, 138, 142, 148, 154
Bilingual education, 48, 53, 54, 55, 56, 72, 84, 107, 157, 158, 169
Bilingualism, 29, 32, 33, 34, 37, 38, 40, 44, 55, 70, 72, 73, 74, 78, 103, 107, 108, 128, 130, 133, 135, 136,

137, 138, 148, 150, 154, 155, 158, 161, 162
Binational, 138, 153
Bronfenbrenner, 66
Children of Immigrants Development in Context (CIDC), 49, 50, 51, 53, 75, 76, 111, 140
Children of Immigrants Longitudinal Study (CILS), 35, 36, 37, 38, 39, 41, 60
Clark and Clark, 143
Current Population Survey (CPS), 3, 13
Demographic trends, US, 3, 4, 21, 24
Dominican immigrants, 11, 12, 14
  Demographic change, 1, 3, 4, 5, 8, 12, 21
  Educational attainment, 12, 13, 20, 22, 149
  Family reunification, 2, 14
  Gender, 149, 150
  Immigration, 11, 14, 15, 16, 21
  Income, 13, 16, 19, 83, 85, 96, 105, 142, 147, 148, 149, 170

Language, 17, 18, 21, 45, 69, 94, 132, 136, 138, 149, 150, 154, 156

Marriage, 14, 15

Migration, 11, 12, 14, 15, 21

Population growth, 11, 20

Poverty, Socioeconomic status, 12, 13, 19, 22

Segregation, 148, 151

Single parent household, 83

Social networks, 14, 15, 18

Stratification, racial/social, 12, 68

Ecological theory, 66, 67, 68, 140, 162

Education, 7, 8, 13, 20, 24, 25, 26, 27, 30, 34, 35, 36, 42, 46, 54, 57, 59, 60, 61, 71, 83, 84, 85, 96, 97, 126, 139, 140, 142, 144, 146, 147, 151, 152, 157, 158, 161, 162, 163, 166, 169, 170

Health, 10, 22, 25, 28, 29, 49, 158

Socioeconomic status, 7, 13, 22, 27, 34, 35, 42, 43, 162

Educational aspirations, 35, 42, 57

Familismo, 145, 146

Feliciano, 40, 41, 42, 60

Foreign-born population, US, 1, 2, 6, 18

Fuligni, 34, 53, 57, 64

García Coll, 18, 27, 34, 49, 120, 153, 157, 159, 161

Gender, 24, 25, 39, 45, 56, 57, 58, 59, 60, 61, 62, 64, 65, 111, 113, 118, 119, 128, 144, 145, 146, 151, 152, 162

Academic achievement, 56, 58, 60, 62, 112, 128, 129, 130, 136, 139, 140, 141, 143, 144

Globalization, 159, 161, 164

Hakuta, 55, 78

Immigrant children, 9, 10, 24, 25, 26, 27, 28, 29, 33, 35, 36, 43, 44, 48, 50, 53, 56, 61, 63, 70, 71, 73, 137, 151, 160, 161

Education, 10, 24, 26, 27, 28, 29, 48, 53, 56, 151, 160

Families, 25, 63, 160

Health, 10, 25, 26

Parents, 25, 26, 27, 160

Poverty, 10, 25, 27, 151

Schools, 28, 29, 161

Immigrant paradox, 51, 52, 53, 63, 64, 133, 135

Immigration Act, 1965, 2, 14

John Berry, 71

Latinos, 2, 3, 4, 5, 6, 7, 8, 10

Demographic change, 3, 4, 5, 6, 8, 10

Educational attainment, 5, 6, 7, 8

Immigration, 2, 3, 8, 10

Language, 4, 6, 7, 9

Population growth, 3, 5, 6, 8

Longitudinal Immigrant Student Adaptation Study (LISA), 45
Lopez, 44, 57, 59, 60, 61, 64, 144, 146, 147
MacCallum & Austin, 86
Machismo, 146
Monroe Doctrine, 17
Multiple worlds theory, 67
Peréa, 2, 18, 34, 49, 153, 157, 159, 161
Phelan, 66, 67
Policy issues, 153, 154, 156, 157, 161, 162, 163, 164
Population changes, 1, 3, 4, 5, 6, 8
Portes, 32, 34, 35, 36, 38, 41, 53, 57, 66, 70, 71, 73, 137, 145, 155, 158, 160
Providence, 11, 12, 16, 17, 18, 19, 20, 21, 22, 138, 147, 148
  Demographic characteristics, 11, 17, 18, 19, 21, 22

Immigrants, 16, 18, 19, 21, 22
Income, 16, 17, 19
Language, 17, 18, 138, 148
Latino community, 17, 18, 138
Poverty, 16, 19, 20, 22
Schools, 20, 21, 148
Unemployment, 16, 17
Rumbaut, 31, 32, 33, 36, 38, 39, 41, 53, 57, 60, 61, 66, 70, 71, 73, 137, 145, 155, 158, 159, 160
Segmented assimilation, 36, 37, 145
Stereotype threat, 143
Structural equation modeling, 77, 85, 86, 87, 88, 89, 92, 116, 119, 120, 132, 133
Suarez-Orozco, 26, 27, 29, 31, 34, 45, 51, 54, 55, 58, 70, 71, 137, 143, 158
Thomas and Collier, 56
Transnational, 15, 68, 153
Waters, 57
Wong-Fillmore, 154, 156, 160